POETS SPEAK OUT

Edited by

Andrew Head

First published in Great Britain in 1998 by
POETRY NOW
1-2 Wainman Road, Woodston,
Peterborough, PE2 7BU
Telephone (01733) 230746
Fax (01733) 230751

All Rights Reserved

Copyright Contributors 1998

HB ISBN 0 75430 547 3
SB ISBN 0 75430 548 1

FOREWORD

Although we are a nation of poetry writers we are accused of not reading poetry and not buying poetry books: after many years of listening to the incessant gripes of poetry publishers, I can only assume that the books they publish, in general, are books that most people do not want to read.

Poetry should not be obscure, introverted, and as cryptic as a crossword puzzle: it is the poet's duty to reach out and embrace the world.

The world owes the poet nothing and we should not be expected to dig and delve into a rambling discourse searching for some inner meaning.

The reason we write poetry (and almost all of us do) is because we want to communicate: an ideal; an idea; or a specific feeling. Poetry is as essential in communication, as a letter; a radio; a telephone, and the main criteria for selecting the poems in this anthology is very simple: they communicate.

Contents

Leading On	T A Napper	1
Waster	Wendy Walker	2
The Dreaded Xmas Party	Terry Cutting	3
Rubberneckers	Emiline McLaughlin	4
Media Control	Cindy Silvester	5
Inequality	P Farhat	6
Ode To The Vexed	Katrina M Greenhalf	7
Others . . .	Jas Singh	8
My Grievances	E Kathleen Jones	9
My Fellow Man	Della M Gander	10
I've Had Enough	Sonia Coneye	11
Calling Cards	Jeannette Facchini	12
Tourists	Emma Howell	13
The Demolition Men	Celia Law	14
Bigotry	Robin Halder	15
Conquered	Anna Walker	16
Banking Blues	Nachelle Chadwick	17
Comet Our World Today	M Hambly	18
Bitter Back	B E Green	19
Smoke	Jayne Williams	20
Meant For Each Other	Jackie Johnson	22
Word Pollution	Carol Mansfield	23
True Thought	Marsha-Lee Barnes	24
Why?	Leann Marie Elkins	25
Eye For Eye	Timm Dorsett	26
Theft	Kathleen Hatton	27
Life Once So Precious	Teresa Booth	28
Explosion	Joyce Parker	29
Indifference	Eileen N Blackmore	30
If I Had My Way	Betty Pearson	31
Brain Injury	Jo Lewis	32
The Critic	Jean Oxley	33
Bite Back	David Goudie	34
Hospital Blues	Susan A Peach	35

Animal Rights	P Tattersall	36
Twilight In-Between	Pauline Joy	37
Getting Even	Jennifer Tuckett	38
Immovable Force	Elizabeth Amy Johns	39
Road Rage	L T Coleman	40
Fox-Hunting	Hayley Ann Edwards	41
Ever Rising And Falling Throughout The Nations	Paul Bartlett	42
In Memoriam . . .	J M Service	43
Litter	David Sheasby	44
Equality, In The Modern World	Anna C Bateson	45
Anthem To The First Drops Of Rain	Dorothy Pope	46
The Zoo	Eileen Shenton	47
Ode To Coventry	R Griffis	48
Drives Me Mad	Numero Uno	49
Africa: The Long Night	R James Hails	50
Boredom	P A Deakin	51
The Slaughterhouse Of Humanity	P V Campbell-Lyons	52
Daisy The Cow In The Flyless Season	S H Smith	53
Evensong	Simon Warren	54
Pre-War Gerrmany	Greta Lesley Marriott	55
Buzz Off	Constance Vera Dewdney	56
The Neighbours From Hell	Anne Polhill Walton	57
A raging nation	Donald L Carey	58
Morons - Belt Up	Penny Brown	60
Litter Bug	Di Bagshawe	61
No, I'm Interested In Babies!	Anna Kemble	62
Freedom Of Speech	Christine Anne Thurling	63
War	Anne Tompsett	64
Waste	Katy Melia	65
Twentieth Century	Ewan Walker	66
Forgiveness!	Steve Hughes	67

Famine	K A Coleran	68
Free For All	Jean Kennedy	69
In Our Own Worlds	Katrina Payne	70
And So I Knock	Dorothy Fisher	71
O Diana!	William Basil McLaughlin	72
Freedom	Jan Trivett	73
Proud OAPs	Patricia Battye	74
Abattoir	Tracie Mark Deakin	75
Perish The Thought	Amanda Allbones	76
Maelstrom	G Richardson	77
Land Of The Free	Sheila Jones	78
Dunblane	Joan Packham	79
Aliens	Billy Kennedy	80
Mr President	Patricia McDonald	81
Consolation	Teresa Dyas	82
Parkinson's	Sheila Barker	83
Chunnel Vision!	Sue Ashdown	84
Like To Like Only	I H Pyves	85
Winning The National Lottery	Nicholas Freville	86
Fame	Paula Fox	87
I Wonder Why	Maisie Roberts	88
The Wall	Kevin Worsnop	89
A Literary Article	G E M Broomhead	90
Legalised Robbery	Carey Whitehead	91
Freedom Of Speech	Esma Wilson Wright	92
Now That's For Me!	J E Alban	93
Unbowed	M Kennedy	94
Freedom Of Speech	Patricia Evans	95
Untitled	Mary Weber	96
Hyde Park, London 300 Miles	Helen Wood	97
Memorials	Graeme Vine	98
The Earth's Cry	Thuha Auda	99
Omagh	Janine Ellis	100
Is God Directing Earthly Life As A Theatrical Play?	Rune Brokstad	101
If The Anti's Get Their Wish	G Hollinsworth	102

Mines	Joan M Hopkins	104
Power Of Speech	Joyce E Williams	105
Democracy	Dianne J Shorthouse	106
Ghost The Bomb	Selina Styles	107
Our Fireman	B D Grindy	108
Benefit Of Clergy	John Hatton Davidson	110
To The Abuser	Eilidh McMillan	111
Does Anybody Care?	A Humphrey	112
Not Honest Anymore	Dave Pearson	113
Why?	Susan Evelyn Churton	114
The Precinct	Shirley Frost	115
Anger	Susan Goldsmith	116
Quest For Peace	Diane Antoniazzi	117
Einstein's Philadelphia	Jean Paisley	118
Famine	Sophie Johnson	119
Legacy	Joan McAvoy	120
Terrorist	Lynda Sumbler	121
Smiling, Young Tony	T Burke	122
Stop!	Kristen Furley	124
Jerusalem - Take Two	Jenni J Moores	125
The Elements	Patricia Flynn	126
Mysterious Predator	Valerie Taber	127
Changing Fear, Changing Freer	David Yates	128
Us, We Are Not Vain	Claire Louise Booker	129
It's Decorum, Sir	Evelyn Leite	130
Into Thin Air	Paul Nicklin	131
Violent Protection	Craig Hetherington	132
The Party	Christine Fraser	133
Our Future	Carrie Anne Hunter	134
A Message From A Dying Planet	Alan Pollard	135
First Time Around - Or What The Robot Said To The Punk	Anne Hadley	136
Inspiration	P J Davies	137
It Comes To Us All!	Hilary Jill Robson	138
Words And Deeds	Jean Bonjour	140

Freewheeling Unspoken Words	Beverley Chipp	141
Our Land	Margaret Sage	142
Packaging	Elizabeth Rigby	143
Mrs Karakusevic	Karen Bradley	144
Justice Denied	Edna M Sarsfield	145
Freedom Of Speech	Muriel Hughes	146
Untitled	Emma Pearce	147
Victory?	Ann Stewart	148

LEADING ON

Why is it a fact in life?
An unfair driving force.
That those who make decisions.
Will whip a willing horse.

They see sincerity and politeness.
As a weakness they can use.
That those who do not answer back.
Are just there to abuse.

They rarely challenge the aggressor.
He will query and complain.
Just chivvy those who take it.
They will absorb the stress and strain.

If you are easy going.
It is very hard to change.
Should you work on your personality.
Even though it may seem strange?

Would it ease the anguish
If your oppressor heard you say
'I am trying hard and doing my best,'
So for . . . my sake go away?'

Life is like a theatre.
For some a mighty con.
The performers work their socks off.
And so many more look on.

T A Napper

WASTER

Who the hell do you think you are?
You think this country owes you a living.
A healthy young man, now in your prime.
One who takes without ever giving.
Five children you have fathered,
without paying a penny for their keep,
this is a typical example,
of as you shall sow you shall reap.
You go to bed early morning,
and get up in the late afternoon.
You manage to smoke forty ciggies a day
and then have the audacity to moan.
Well I'm going to tell you something,
I've worked fifty two hours a week,
whilst bringing my daughter up, alone.
Us, the State did not keep.
We did not have money for luxuries,
what we had we worked bloody hard for.
We also had love and morals
and that stopped us from being poor.
So get off your backside and look for a job
and invest in a packet of condoms.
Go and work a forty-hour week
and help solve the country's problems.

Wendy Walker

THE DREADED XMAS PARTY

It's Christmas in the office and the same shit every year
Miserable sods will come to life on just a whiff of beer
They acknowledge you for one day out of three hundred and sixty five
In between the festive seasons they don't care if you're alive
No Christmas bonus once again just a meal in some naff place
With portions fit for insects - not enough to stuff your face
The boss will have some wine before he slurs a feeble joke
He tries to make us all believe that he's just a normal bloke
We'll talk of work and little else because 'boring' is what you are
While I fidget with the cutlery just longing for my car
Don the paper hats from crackers as if we're clever and unique
The waiter will smile in sympathy - he'll see it fifty times this week
I'll make small talk with a cretin who I would gladly kill and stuff
I've seen their bloody face all year and by now I've had enough
Office bimbos wrapped in tinsel with plastic antlers on their heads
Waving mistletoe at salesmen who want to get them into bed
Faces redden with the wine while I sit in sober stare
Dreaming of my local pub and praying to be there
The boss will spout the pep talk and every time it's just the same
'You're so important to the team!' - but he still forgets my name
Tipsy women come a-groping glasses swinging on their chains
Do they think that men are roused by drunken hags with tiny brains?
You may well be important but I really couldn't care
Why don't you snog yourself a pay rise and please don't touch me there
People start to mention leaving and I'm the first one to the door
My mind is bent on genocide I just can't take it any more
When the *agadoos* have finished and I reach the cold night air
I raise my eyes towards the heavens to offer up a silent prayer
I thank dear God for Jesus, yes I thank him for his son
And I bless his cotton socks because he only had the one.

Terry Cutting

Rubberneckers

Picture the scene, it's one we know too well,
Crawling down the M25, frustrated as hell.
But the reason why I lose my temper
Is not the delay, but the tasteless rubberneckers.

Those of us unfortunate enough to be in a crash
Deserve concern, for an experience that harsh,
Not those cars who slow down to see all the better,
Those immoral and shameful rubberneckers.

I thought days of public hangings were left in the past,
When crowds would watch transfixed, whilst people breathed their last,
I thought mankind hated carnage, but my tastes must differ,
To those of the savage, gore-loving rubberneckers.

But when their rubbernecks snap, and staring eyes glaze over,
They will have the close up view they have always dreamed for,
And in the wreckage of their cars, while in death they lie,
A new breed of rubberneckers crawl, oh so slowly, by . . .

Emiline McLaughlin

MEDIA CONTROL

Thin is in.
Wear this style,
Designer labels of course!
Eat this.
Drink that.
Watch this.
Enough!
Media control.
On and on
The media declares
What you should wear.
Glittering Hollywood styles
Show beauty,
Based on shallowness.
Why can't we choose,
The things we want to do
Without media control?
So, I buy clothes
Without media control?
So I buy clothes
Without designer labels
And I am the unique one.
Don't stop and glare
And think I'm not cool
For I am not the one
Under media control.

Cindy Silvester

INEQUALITY

Class division
Socially created

Creating inequalities,
prejudices,
among those on the rung
higher up than those below.

What difference
does a sum of coins
and notes make

When society cannot
get on as a whole

When a person's
clothes and possessions
are more important
than the content
of their hearts?

P Farhat

ODE TO THE VEXED

It takes more effort frowning
Than it does to cast a smile,
On those who would bewilder
In attempt to then beguile.
So if you face a joker
Trying to tease you with intent,
Free a smile and rise politely
Leave the frowning up to them!

Katrina M Greenhalf

OTHERS...

Often interfere - step in.
Nose.
Poke.
Pry.

Unwittingly, cross the mark.
Boundary.
Line.
Mine.

Unknowingly, vex me,
Irritate -
Annoy -
Anger me!

Do not interfere with me!

I am my own.
Take views,
Advice, suggestions -
Throw them at the tides!

If they frown once more,
From their cultural isle to mine,
I shall scream!

Leave.
Me.
Alone.

Jas Singh

My Grievances

As a seaside resident it makes me angry to view,
All the litter left around by visitors who
Are indifferent to our attractive promenade.
Not using bins provided for their rubbish to discard
Ice-cream tubs, cartons, cans and newspapers.
In sea breeze fresh cutting merry capers,
As along the front they chase one another
Whilst angrily I watch, rage trying to smother

Then there's the dog owner furtively looking around,
Before allowing their pet to foul garden and ground.
Such people should be asked how *they* would feel,
Returning home with dog excreta from toe to heel.
Maybe a police summons would bring then to book,
Making them change their habits and also outlook

And lastly the vandals who take delight,
In waiting until comes the darkness of night,
To cause damage to seafront and town shop,
When no one's near to make them stop,
Smashing shelter and shop windows, leaving no trace
Of those responsible for such havoc and disgrace.
If only they could be caught, made to pay for damage done
Such action would bring relief to everyone.

E Kathleen Jones

MY FELLOW MAN

Thoughtless smokers who flout all the rules
Thundering stereos in cars roaring by
Football fans drunk abroad, acting like fools
Such are the things that make me heave and sigh.

Ignorant neighbours with bonfires ablaze
When you in your garden sit out
Why do they always choose very hot days?
To annoy everybody, no doubt!

Taxi drivers sounding horns late at night
Rather than knocking on doors
Parents of bullies who start the school fights
And if you complain - the fault's yours.

Ghouls who set out to drive to a crash
To watch all the debris and pain
Drivers who walk free after a smash
Even if they're killed or maimed.

People who add up your clothes at a glance
Without knowing anything's worth
Bosses who will not give workers a chance
And treat their suggestions with mirth.

People who knock those with real success
And have nothing in them but spite
Perhaps they pray the balance will redress
And then they can gloat they were right.

Do you recognise yourself in the above?
Are you one of the ones who're to blame?
Try and treat fellow humans with respect and love
Eventually, you'll get back the same.

Della M Gander

I'VE HAD ENOUGH

I'm a long-suffering daughter, mother and wife
Football I've lived with all my life
Football they eat, drink and sleep
It's on our tele for most of the week
Demanding and forceful I've always lacked
Well I've had enough, time to bite back
I'm making demands like it or not
I'm sick of football, you've had your lot
When world cup fever was in the air
In our house, I just wasn't there
Conversation was limited to *'What a great goal!'*
Screaming shouting and a whole lot more
For over four weeks, all were hooked
Seats in our lounge had to be booked
Then when I thought I've moaned within reason
It's now the start of the football season
Well I've had enough, time to bite back
My blood's reached boiling, this is no act
Having a father, husband and son
I'm always outvoted three to one.
So now I'm biting back, making a stand
Taking control, making demands
There's more to life than football, okay
And I've had my share of football I'd say
So I've had enough, time to bite back
Demanding, forceful, I think I'm on the right track.

Sonia Coneye

CALLING CARDS

Like many more I find it hard
When doggies leave their calling card
But what is even worse, it's true -
Substances sticking to my shoe.

Don't blame the dogs for they don't know
Or even have a place to 'go'
Some owners just don't seem to care
When Rover 'does it' over there.

This dirt, it sometimes even cleaves
Or hides among the autumn leaves
But summer, winter, autumn, spring
This stuff is an obnoxious thing.

Please ban it! Banish! Or outlaw
What we now have to watch out for
Till then I'll walk with careful tread
Looking down, not straight ahead!

Jeannette Facchini

TOURISTS

Brash, overweight women,
With flesh constricted
Into moist, white plastic shoes,
Gawp inanely,
Shrieking for photos
As they contort their globular bodies.
Red, sticky children
Drone incessant as sirens
For souvenir pencils
And more ice cream
To smear down their already
Multi-flavoured T-shirts,
Shattering the stillness
Of the monumental air
As they clamber irreverently
Upon megalithic formations,
Oblivious to the mystique,
The beauty, the peace.
Tourists
Forever in search of the eternal snapshot
And elusive ice cream.

Emma Howell

THE DEMOLITION MEN

A group of men declared it must come down,
This unsafe building painted brown,
But the residents are concerned about the mess,
There will be just a little, the men confess,
We will spray with water to keep down the dust,
Every time the bricks fall and make a gust,
They also mentioned the noise and the din,
We will keep that down too, they lied with a grin.

Fences were put up, the noise wasn't bad,
The residents believed them, how very sad,
Then came Monday morning and the machines moved it,
And you have never heard such a terrible din,
Bangs and crashes as bricks fell to the ground,
Closed windows all around to keep out the sound,
Clouds of red dust fly up in the air,
Those demolition men didn't really care.

The residents complain, but it falls on deaf ears,
Bosses listen, then laugh, over a few beers,
The mess and the noise goes on and on,
It will not stop till the demo men have gone,
The only peace they have is at the dead of night,
But the building's almost gone, out of sight,
They sigh with relief as the machines move out,
Now at least they can hear each other shout.

Now the residents believed that was the end,
But the news out today will drive them round the bend,
Half a dozen houses to be built on the land,
How much more upheaval do they think we can stand,
Cement mixers and lorries trundling in and out,
'Why us?' they say 'What's it all about?'
The builders are bad enough with their noise and mayhem,
But they're not half as bad as those bloody demo men.

Celia Law

BIGOTRY

I enter the reception door to the Engineering works where
                                        I have an appointment.
The receptionist ushers me into the Technical Manager's office.
Passionately, I put forward the benefits of Metalastik's
                                        engineering products
And their unique appeal to his company,
Leaving detailed literature on his particular wants.
Patiently, I listen to his needs and woes,
Thereby ascertaining that a current late delivery will seriously
                                        jeopardise his business.
Therefore, I tell him that I will not leave until I sort out his problem.
Despite the fact that I will be late for my next meeting and
As a Sales Engineer, my sole duty is to take orders.
I ring the Manageress in charge and ask her if a solution can be found to
                                        this immediate problem.
Ten minutes later, a solution is found and I gain next year's
                                        worth of orders.
As I am about to leave, the phone rings and he replies to the
                                        Commercial Director,
'I am currently with the WOG.'
Bile rises to my throat and I begin to see red.
Rapidly, I make my farewells.
As I leave I think to myself,
That I am being judged solely on my melanin content as well as;
Would my Caucasian colleagues have helped him out as much as I had?

Robin Halder

CONQUERED

How can people treat you
as if you weren't living, breathing,
allowing us to be?

Willingly tormenting you
for the sake of a childish game,
dangling on a string.

Unable to wait for nature
they hunt you down,
simply for pleasure.

Adults, children, all alike,
abusing you with your own weapon.
How would they like it done to them?

Anna Walker

BANKING BLUES

Pleasant, polite.
Me - uptight.
Numbers, sums, mandates,
I'm in a terrible state.

Did I make the error?
I feel my tremor.
It was the Students' Loans Co,
I'm so relieved to know.

You won't charge me, no way?
He's not authorised to say.
Another phone call next week,
I think it's a blooming cheek.

No apology, niceness or sorry,
No consideration for my lost time or worry.
After all it's all just numbers,
The things that push me towards slumber!

Nachelle Chadwick

COMET OUR WORLD TODAY

God has given us a fortune
To treat with respect
But know we take it for granted
All those plants we planted
There's got to be a way
To comet our world today.

The sun is burning brighter
The world is getting lighter
One more chance is all we need
To show our love that's all we plead
To see the world disappear
It makes me feel so unhappy and blue.

I never imagined it will be this way
To see the world in such pain
There has to be a way
To unite the human race
I don't understand because some of us
Don't even wonder and some just don't care
Lord, we believe in you now
Just tell us how to stop the pain.

M Hambly

BITE BACK

There are many things which do infuriate me,
Which as I grew older I'd choose not to see.
But whereas one can avert their eyes,
some of today's speech I heard with surprise.

The beautiful English language that many of us cherish,
Is blurred by younger generation with much relish.
It's such a pity for to sensitive ears,
It brings uppermost very many fears.

One can't blame the youngsters, if they're never taught,
That the art of good speaking can never be bought.
But a well-spoken person will always go far,
No matter of what background they are.

I do not refer to artificial speech,
Which many these days feel they should teach.
But good, plain English understood by all,
Not the moment words are uttered, a person from grace does fall.

B E Green

SMOKE

Smoke gets in your hair
and in your clothes
It gets in your eyes
and up your nose
You breathe it in
goes down your throat
You start to cough
Then you choke
It gives bronchitis, emphysema
and cancer
You lose all your friends
You don't care a fraction
You enjoy the feeling
of letting go and relaxing
Your fingers go yellow
your breath starts to smell
and a few years later
you don't feel too well
You can't walk uphill
like you used to when younger
You can't breathe properly
You won't last much longer.
You go to hospital
They give you the answer
You have a disease
a form of lung cancer
Cancer's a killer
as you well know
but you didn't believe them
when they told you so
You have a lung transplant
but it's no good
because the cancer
has spread through the blood
Your body is raging
and flaming inside

No more can be done
They've tried and tried
The damage was done when you lit your first fag
because you and your friends thought it a wag.
You wouldn't have done if you knew how it looked
suddenly you know you're truly hooked
You are addicted to nicotine and tar
and you know it's gone too far
You end up a pile of old bones
and a name carved on the stones
That's what happens when you start to smoke
You carry on, you haven't a hope
but you never believed them when
They told you so.

Jayne Williams

MEANT FOR EACH OTHER

If there's one thing that really gets up my nose
Apart from my finger, that is,
It's *Blind Date* and couples on match-making shows
Pretending to be on a quiz.

I don't think the answers are funny at all
Like the questions, they're far too rehearsed,
And if one more contestant pretends to be *cool*
I think my suspenders will burst!

No one's clever enough to ad-lib like that
Especially on TV
With a see-through short dress or peculiar hat
The girls don't look real to me.

The guys either act like macho machines
Or else they're a *bit of a lad*
Larger than life they appear on my screen
And I think 'Get a life' and 'How sad!'

The winner's the one with the naffest replies
And whether you're chosen or you are the chooser
Each word is untrue, they're all porky pies
And to me *every* one is a loser.

Jackie Johnson

WORD POLLUTION

What foul-mouthed monsters
Stalk the streets
Of today's society;
From their lips so often come
Blasphemies, obscenities
Which pain and cause extreme offence,
Freedom of speech, abused, misused,
Product of enlightened age?
Heard and seen on screen and page
Invade to cheapen and degrade.
Is there no limit, no restraint?
Has word pollution come to stay
Like so much filth portrayed today?

It is possible to find
Cleanliness and decency,
While words well used will yet convey
Wholesome pleasure, healthy thought
That will not grate upon the ear
Or repulse and vex the eye,
But can uplift, enhance, inspire,
Is it not too much to seek
To raise the tone of uttered speech,
Before it sinks beyond recall
To gutter level totally.

Carol Mansfield

TRUE THOUGHT

I search for truth, dignity, honesty and love . . . !
Where is the opening?
I stand on top of my bed looking down upon the globe.
Why does she still cry for her mother?
Someone tell her there is another.
Don't tell me the sky is purple, when it's blue.
Am I blind . . . ? Or is it my choice to avoid all the void?
In the beginning the spirit of God moved upon the face of the waters
And the earth was without spoil.
Do you get it . . . ? Pathetic isn't it?
Or maybe ironic, that we've all forgotten the beginning.
But we are never to forget that a beginning has an end.
Did you know . . . ?
It was God in Christ, who came to reconcile the world?
I forget you then, in your stiff suit, alongside your stiff neck
Drinking Chardonnay, eating caviar, walking on your belly
And ruling what's not yours.
Can you imagine when all is taken away? Money man - *power* -
You've created your own nuclear destruction.
Why do you lie . . . ? What is love . . . ?
I stand alone, I am an individual born without a twain.
To write and perform a number one hit,
Is like playing in a doll's house. - Have you got a doll's house?
And to write, produce and direct a movie
Is like baking a pineapple upside down pudding,
Do you know how to bake one?
Tell me the truth . . . I require the truth *only* . . .
I am angry, for I am innocent, to the charge that is held against me -
But if God is for me, who can be against me . . . ? Who . . . ? You?
In the revelation all is revealed - Revelation being a revolution.
To such things my eyes are opened.
To live and tell . . . is my purpose.

Marsha-Lee Barnes

Why?

Why so many dumb lies?
What's the point?
What's the bother?
Why do they have to try and impress each other?
Secrets are secrets just between us,
what happens, happens that's all no more
so why lie add more, what's the big fuss?
Stuff their egos, why try to be tough
it shouldn't be like that, how can you trust?
Trust is important,
a definite must,
without it there's nothing
you mustn't break trust.
So why tell lies?
They only bring anger and pain
and then comes the shame.
How can you love without trust?
Are they all the same?
Do they lie again and again?
Is it part of their nature
or just the way they are?
Why must they impress each other
and make up such lies?
Maybe everything is just one big story
does love and trust really exist?
I think maybe not!

Leann Marie Elkins

EYE FOR EYE

Why are we so self-righteous?
Horrified by a heinous c rime against so many innocent,
And then with the same breath,
Blast our reply on others so our anger we can vent,
Surely an eye for an eye and a tooth for a tooth,
Does not bring back the dead,
Can we not turn the other cheek and seek a peaceful response?
Humble the perpetrators in Ghandi's way instead.

Timm Dorsett

THEFT

Torture no animals for me
To haunt with unavailing cry,
Nor steal, with cruel-clever hands,
Their right to live - my right to die.

If pain should in the future come
To rack this coward flesh of mine,
It may be I should not disdain
The partial peace of anodyne.
I am no saint, to welcome pain;
But cause no pain, to banish mine.

So steal no extra time for me,
If, dying, I am unafraid,
Knowing no trusting animal
Has borne my pain, and died betrayed.

Kathleen Hatton

LIFE ONCE SO PRECIOUS

Life once thought of as being so precious,
Now seems to be disposable, people show
So little respect for it.
We are shocked no longer at murders,
So routine have they become.
War is a daily occurrence, yet
Unless it directly impinges on our life,
We are left relatively unmoved, unaffected.
Thousands are killed by natural disasters,
Tornadoes, floods and earthquakes
Yet the aid we send is selective.
Helping only those in whom we have a vested interest.
Aircraft carrying hundreds fail,
Plummeting earthwards, landing in pieces.
Our news reports, factual, unemotional,
Moved only if any of its passengers are English.
Criminals are judged by the law courts,
Removed from society by the penal system.
Citizens, over drinks, in the privacy of homes,
Partake in idle chatter, pass judgement,
Ensure they offend, not again, exterminate them.
Unborn children, in silence are extinguished,
Their loss kept secret, shame prevents publication.
Am I innocent of these affairs?
Are my hands clean?
I believe so,. but then again, I argue, is this so?
Does not my passivity condone these actions?
Why do I not make a protest against the injustice?
I fear I, like many are guilty.
My hands are soiled.

Teresa Booth

EXPLOSION

What makes me bitter
is unwanted litter
where it need not be!
Can't people see
The mess it makes,
The time it takes
To gather it in
And put in the bin
By an innocent carer
Who couldn't be fairer
In keeping neat
Her part of a street!
We should all have a heart
And make a firm start
To keep things in order
Within our own border:
Best leave subject there,
Before I simply go spare!

Joyce Parker

INDIFFERENCE

The sufferings of the soul are unknown to passers-by,
Who heedlessly ignore them, hearing not the silent cry
That rises from the inmost depths of one in deep despair,
Who raises hopeless eyes, beseeching in unuttered prayer.

A gesture of understanding; a friendly human touch;
A tender word of sympathy, would mean so very much.
For apathy and callousness just emphasise the grief
Of each despondent soul which yearns for comfort and relief.

Eileen N Blackmore

IF I HAD MY WAY

I'd ban from the theatre, cinema, show
Everyone listed here below.
Head bobbers, nodders, whisperers, talkers,
Coughers and sniffers. Anyone raucous.
Clever Dicks explaining the scenes.
Women wearing tight blue jeans.

People rustling paper wraps.
Noisy children perched on laps.
Fiddlers, fidgets, tappers of feet.
Hoggers of arm rests between each seat.
Shedders of footwear, boot or shoe.
Wearers of hats obscuring the view.

Tut tutters and moaners. People who snore.
Anyone who's seen the show before.
Everyone late or anxious to go
Before the ending of the show.
Banish them all. Let them be gone.
Leave in the theatre an audience of one.

Betty Pearson

BRAIN INJURY

At first we trusted in their planned support
Naively thought the so called experts knew
Just how to help, advise and guide us through
But all they did was constantly resort
To shuffling paper - shelving our concerns
Because, quite clearly, no one had a clue
Precisely what to recommend or do
Except insist the rules were on their terms

And then, as caring parents, we were dealt
A hand not ever possible to win
Though played at length, whilst burying within
The agonising trauma we both felt.
And still we fight the system, but in vain
Caught up in webs of bureaucratic tape
Still pressing the establishment to make
Improved provision for the injured brain

Jo Lewis

THE CRITIC

It pains me, dear, to interfere;
You know it's not my way;
But if you'll kindly lend an ear,
There's something I must say.
That skull and crossbones on your coat
Gives Mummikins the creeps;
Likewise the tattoo of a goat
That from your cleavage peeps.
I wonder if the navel ring
Was such a good idea.
It really is a horrid thing
And painful too, I fear.
Why won't you get a proper job
To help you up the ladder?
Now, don't tell me to shut my gob,
Or say you're getting madder!
Why must you use that green hair dye?
It gives the wrong idea.
The neighbours think you're mad and I
Am disappointed, dear!
Why can't you be like other girls
of your age, sweet and coy,
With pouting lips and pretty curls
And some well-mannered boy?
I'd love to see you married off,
With babies round you knees.
No! Put down that Kalashnikov!
Don't pull the trigger, *please!*

Jean Oxley

BITE BACK

Often we meet people walking in the street
Who suddenly turn around and trample on your feet.
They never say 'I'm sorry for treading on your toes.'
Bad manners are a feature now, no matter where one goes.

Spring doors into offices, shops and clearing banks,
With courtesy you hold them but many don't say thanks.
Often times you hold the doors in many of those places,
It makes you feel a naughty urge to slam them in their faces.

In superstores you sometimes feel you'd like to shout a volley
Because they block the passages with their loaded trolley.
And when you say 'Excuse me please, I'm trying to get through,'
They look at you as if to say, who the hang are you?

Our footpaths now are cycling tracks, our roads like 'Silverstone'.
It is true what the song says - 'You'll Never Walk Alone'.
So if you can't beat them join them and get yourself a bike
And put terror in pedestrians and save yourself a hike.

I don't know where we are going in this present state
With so much poor manners to cause us so much hate.
It is sad to see our populace bearing little thought,
It's reflective on the home life and what Mum and Daddy taught.

It takes all kinds of people to form a worldly place,
Some we hold in honour, others in disgrace.
We seem to see the bad in folk, it precedes the good,
The ways of men are awkward, never fully understood.

David Goudie

HOSPITAL BLUES

Waiting room blues
And miserable faces
Arms and legs
All waiting for repair
Patience wearing thin as
Nurses rush hither and thither
Trying to keep mounting queues down
While patients resign themselves
To hours of waiting and boredom
And hours of unorganised chaos.
Ill-patient children bored with sitting still,
Noisy, squeaking wheelchairs
All join in the din
Making you grind your teeth.

Precious time wasted by bad organisation
And the lack of qualified staff.
Time which could be better spent
Enjoying fresh air and sunshine that is
Nowadays so rare and precious.
No room to sit,
Car parks overflowing,
Tempers fraying as waiting time increases,
Relief when it's time for you to be treated
And it's time to go home.

Susan A Peach

ANIMAL RIGHTS

There's talk of bringing back again
a trade that almost died,
The killing of our furry friends
to rob them of their hide.
Our animals are dying
in torment and in pain
All for the sake of fashion
for vanity and gain.

Their little limbs are broken
in traps so cruelly set,
There will be no escape for them
they won't elude the net.
There's some born in captivity
who never roam the earth
Enclosed in tiny cages
right from their day of birth.

Our animals weren't born to suffer
in this unnatural way
Deprived of all their beauty
for humans to display.
If only man would realise
that animals have rights too
The right to live their lives in peace
the same as me and you.

How can we ever justify
the wearing of these furs?
On animals they do belong
for they are rightly theirs,
I often sit and wonder
would this carnage still go on?
If they could only answer back
and say *'Leave us alone.'*

P Tattersall

TWILIGHT IN-BETWEEN

He who knows a truth or lie
From the twilight in-between,
Is a man I'd dearly like to meet,
For to me, it strangely seems,
That the blackest lie
Slowly, day by day,
Turns into the rosy pinks
And the pearly greys
Of the twilight in-between.

Pauline Joy

GETTING EVEN

I don't think there's anything more rewarding,
anything more satisfying or better,
than venting your anger and hurt and concern,
with paper and pen and letter.

It's true what they say, I heartily agree,
the pen is mightier than the sword,
especially if published and distributed to friends
of the hurtful person you've floored.

There's no need to worry, I won't spill the beans,
this time, retaliation I've spawned,
but push me too far and next time or the next
I'll snap. So be nice. You've been warned.

Jennifer Tuckett

IMMOVABLE FORCE

He believes . . . and it is so;
What matter, though it's not?
If he believes, so must it be -
No justice here, but painfully
I've learned 'tis best forgot.

He disbelieves . . . and it's not so;
What matter, though it be?
If he disbelieves, then it is not -
No justice still, but well I know
Again . . . 'tis best forgot.

Elizabeth Amy Johns

ROAD RAGE

Road rage, the modern aberration
That changes all the joy of simple driving,
Making its own rules and complexities.
An aggravated nightmare of contriving.

To press advantages in every scheme
Exaggerating each new move you've shown.
Pin-pointing all your faults and weaknesses,
And always your mistake, and not their own.

To quit their vehicle in anger, should
You hesitate at traffic lights, and then
You realise it's just a trickle light,
And you are able to proceed again

Sometimes a punch-up seems a form of violence,
To stress the point of view that they intend,
With knife, or other weapon on occasion,
To make their point of view, or gain their end.

Intolerance can never be a virtue,
Nor be sustained in each, or every case.
A theory based on brutal pure aggression
This torpid state of mind, a sheer disgrace.

L T Coleman

Fox-Hunting

Thumping hooves,
Barking dogs,
Thumping hearts,
Running through fog.

A man and his horse,
A fox and his life,
Sharp jagged teeth,
Cutting flesh like a knife.

A jumbled mumble,
Excited hounds,
Once lived a fox,
Now hunters proud

It's known as a sport,
A sport they say,
A poor fearful animal,
Its life just torn away.

Hayley Ann Edwards

EVER RISING AND FALLING THROUGHOUT THE NATIONS

Pop stars, film stars,
Football stars
Too -
Dream vehicles for what others aspire to do;

Widespread adulation,
Throughout the nation -
Ever risking public frisking and flagulation;

Genuine 'Saints',
And those that ain't . . .

Press hounds in search of story,
Unknowns in search of glory;
Constant reinvention,
To stay in contention;
Tabloid press sensationalisation,
Throughout the nation -
Mocking
Those that are not shocking;

Blight
Of being required to be 'whiter than white';
Confusion of when 'bad',
So 'really, really, bad' -
As to really be quite 'good',
And what really should
To be projected as appropriate guide
For the many,
By PR niche marketing, publicity, and telly -
The few supposedly speaking for many,
So as to beg -
Imperative questions about the 'chicken and egg' . . .

Paul Bartlett

In Memoriam . . .

With mordant words is biter bit,
And in the writing I have writ . . .
No prisoners my pen shall take,
And you who wished me ill will quake . . .

For all who caused me pain and fear
Shall find themselves remembered here;
Their deeds writ large on every page,
Recording for all time my rage . . .

For hatred, like love, is a curse
To live with, for good - or for worse;
Catharsis brings its bitter pain
Before sweet peace takes hold again.

Sometimes I fill my every page
With fear and anger, pain and rage;
Sometimes I wage a war with peace,
And pray the battle shall not cease.

Sometimes sweet conflict fills my mind -
And peace itself becomes unkind.
The war I rage must run its course,
And every truth writ large endorse.

Remorseless, I cannot forgive
Those with no remorse to give;
And they who sought to do me ill
Shall find my pen will strike and kill . . .

J M Service

LITTER

I hate to see litter,
Lying on the ground,
Some are sensible and pick it up
And some just kick it around.

Litter can be dangerous,
You may cut yourself on a tin,
And before you really know it,
The hospital you'll be in.

There are such things as litter bins
To put your rubbish in
So please put your rubbish
In the nearest litter bin.

So can I ask you please
To take your litter home
So Britain will be a tidy place
And no-one can ever moan.

David Sheasby

EQUALITY, IN THE MODERN WORLD

Our child's bright,
They could be pulled down.
I believe in supporting local schools,
Just not ours.
You can be tarnished by encounter,
I've heard the stories,
I know what goes on in places like that.

Don't sit there,
You could catch something.
It's a highly contagious disease,
They should be isolated.
And I know how it starts,
Filthy people contract these things.

I abhor racism.
But rumour has it,
That without immigrants,
There wouldn't even be unemployment!
And they live in squalor,
All road sweeps and toilet scrubbers,
Not nice families.

Like a herd of wilder-beasts the masses are ignorant,
Followers of fads and fashions,
Striving for superiority.
They spread their beliefs,
And like that one match carelessly dropped,
The whole field burns.

Anna C Bateson

ANTHEM TO THE FIRST DROPS OF RAIN

Come, Rain, my friend, and drive inside
All noise-polluting hooligans:
'Gardeners' with head-splitting
Machines, assorted organs,
Car worshippers with vacuum cleaner,
Power hose, and those with radios
Outside, and shouting kids on skates:
The deaf, the insensitive,
The downright rude.

Wash them away indoors.
Restore my lebensraum
To me,
Your gentle but effective self
The only remedy.
And then I'll venture out again
Into the tranquil air
To walk, inhabit and enjoy
A world that's also mine.

Your droplets on my face
Exhilarate. Cool wetness
Steams the perfumed earth
Of therapeutic natural scents.
Flowers drink and thrive
As I do in the grateful quiet
Breathing the needed peace.
Come, rain my friend and mend
My health to gladness.

Dorothy Pope

THE ZOO

Come and see the animals
That once went two by two,
When Noah built his famous Ark
And watched the sky grow very dark
While rain replaced the dew.

Come and see the animals
That braved that earthly flood,
Then walked the earth, when nicely dry,
All free to roam and safely lie
Just anywhere they would.

Come and see the animals
Now kept within these bars,
So confining there's barely room
To pace about, while people loom
And gawk as though at 'stars'.

Come and see the animals
Who round their cages pace,
Whose minds are in a dreadful state
And know not what will be their fate
At whim of 'human' race.

Come and see the animals,
That's what 'they'd' have us do,
But I, for one, can't bear their cries
Or see the torment in their eyes,
I just can't stand the zoo.

Come and see the animals
And help them in their woe,
Though some are saved ere species lost
It's all at most enormous cost,
Man will forever owe.

Eileen Shenton

ODE TO COVENTRY

No sweeter city in the land
        fined and crafted by artisan hand
spawning craftsmen through the ages
        beauty and legend fill historic pages.

Cathedral with spires standing high
        pointing fingers to the sky
from whence would come devastation
        to lay her low in altercation.

That she would arise in greater glory
        to carry on the immortal story
was the prayer for those who cared,
        to all whose roots she shared.

Alas our hopes began to fade
bulldozer - pick, pneumatic spade
        ripped and gouged into history
with mad abandoned irreverie.

We who knew and loved her well
        with only memories left to tell
of pre-architect and planners orgy are now
left with concrete jungles in our story.

But I for one regret my languor
        in not voicing loud, my silent anger
and in my failure not to see
        the rape of our beloved Cofas-Tree.

R Griffis

DRIVES ME MAD

The standard of the drivers
Leave a lot to be desired
I'm sure that many of them
Are either drunk or maybe tired

Impatient is their middle name
They must be down or blue
Always pushing up the front
Instead of joining in the queue.

They're riding round in flashy cars
So fast it would appear
How do they drive with a mobile phone
Makes you wonder how they steer.

Doing deals along the motorway
Looks like they're trying to fly
The standard of our drivers
It makes you want to cry.

Numero Uno

AFRICA: THE LONG NIGHT

Oh Africa! When will your long night end?

Measure the night not in passage of time
but in count of the coup d'etat;
tell it in terms of the generals
as they flaunt their peacock's plumes;
count it in the bloodshed
by soldiers rampant and cruel;
count it in the martial law
clung to by power-drunk men;
count slaughter of infants,
the weak and infirm;
count rape of women and girls;
count neglect of crops, thus famine;
count terror, flight and disease;
count shattered limbs from numberless mines,
the maiming and blinding and pain;
count, too, the stirring of tribal hate,
the guilt of elders and chiefs;
count then the cost of your ghastly night
in a nightmare you've set not to end.

And seeking to gain, the politically apt;
add political graft for power;
count perversion of truth,
deception of youth and rigging of the polls.
Then mourn the death of democracy,
so tragic: it's hardly begun.

Is it not true, while lions fight, that
the jackal runs off with the prize?

Oh Africans, when will you end your long night!

R James Hails

BOREDOM

Boredom can take you in many ways
It can last an hour or maybe days
It can feed on your mind when you're feeling weak
I feel so edgy, life's a cheat

I have things to do but can't seem to think
Alone and bored, I feel a freak
I could do the ironing or have a long bath
I'm not in the mood, too bored to laugh

I sit and sigh and wonder what's next
I feel so bored, oh! what the heck
There's people to see and things I could do
Being bored is a waste, not for me or you

Sometimes it can't be helped
When your mind wanders around
This feeling of being empty
No need to make no sounds

Being bored makes you tired, no energy left
I must do something, create a mess
Can't wait for work, there's so much to do
Too busy to be bored, how about you?

P A Deakin

The Slaughterhouse Of Humanity

War is a kind of madness
that infects men's minds.
The lust for aggression
created by rampant genes
inherent in the male psyche.
A poisonous, destructive element.

Eyes blaze with anticipation
and a need for gratification
of the fighting instinct,
in realms where;
power and lethal tenacity
reign supreme.

Obscene, the imbecility
of mass destruction.
Pitted shells replacing edifices
erected by loving hands,
intent on contributing to civilisation,
instead of yielding to base brutality,
and a distorted form of hedonism and carnage.

The posturing and strutting
smothering gentleness and beauty,
in a welter of bloody, mangled corpses,
and shattered structures.
Where women and children weep
in despairing hopelessness
at men's stupidity.

P V Campbell-Lyons

DAISY THE COW IN THE FLYLESS SEASON

October brings the season of relief:
Now, for a little while, the autumn sun
Intoxicates the mind against such grief
As gathers in the gloom when day is done.
Today, no irritating insect stings,
Nor swarms, with dismal clouds, before the eyes,
And clear as glass, the soaring skylark sings
Her late lament in chalky downland skies -
Or sings for joy? A paean to Him who made
These verdant hills and yonder shining sea,
And little heavens in pools of sylvan shade -
The legacy of trembling leaf and tree?
This Sussex tapestry of sheep-cropped down,
The purple passion of the wind-blown flower,
The year's sublime reprise in russet-brown:
There's almost rapture in this transient hour.

Then man, the wolf, descends upon the fold
In rabid avarice on smothering wings;
And cow and sheep to destiny are sold -
Exploited partners in man's scheme of things.
Daisy goes, too, with sad and wondering eyes,
Envisaging her fate with bated breath,
And grimly greets in strange, vermilion skies,
The locust-bearing harbinger of death.
Remembering her radiant hour she goes,
The hapless victim of consumer will:
Her only comfort at life's cruel close -
A swarm-free season on a sun-kissed hill.

S H Smith

EVENSONG

The way everyone evokes God
As though God
Had anything to do
With blowing up other people,
Their property.
The men of God
Always capitalise
On the misfortune of others.
Personally
I'd send God
With his entourage
Into oblivion.
Without him
People'd manage fine,
Without someone in a dog collar
Constantly gloating
At our misfortune.
Making us look outside ourselves
For what
In truth
Is a part of us all.
Without God
We'd knuckle under,
Accept life for what it is,
Make a go
Of getting on
With each other.
Out of a job,
Servants of the church
Would be like us.

Simon Warren

Pre-War Germany

Chancellor

The economy, it's a real mess,
Oh competition is the best.
We will start a war in Europe,
Then destroy the monied Jews,
We will be the top dogs,
And always have new shoes.

How to save money and compete.

Now Fritz how is the work going,
I've killed half a million Jews,
But Lance has bettered me,
With very different views.

He's rounded up the disabled,
The blind, deaf and dumb,
He's gassed the total lot,
It's saved us a tidy sum.

Greta Lesley Marriott

BUZZ OFF

I booked a seat on a '125'
That's a train that travels fast.
Use British Rail the adverts say
And so the die was cast.

I took my seat and settled down,
As soon as the journey began -
I realised I was seated
By a very busy man.

His papers all were scattered
Across a table meant for four,
He obviously had work to do,
Didn't mean to be a bore.

And then it started - a piercing 'bleep'
'Hello Charlie, how are you?'
We didn't mean to listen
But what else could we do?

There were 'bleeps' and 'buzzes'
All down the train,
As other phones called in,
I don't know how I kept my cool, it really was a din.

In future when I travel,
And want to read a book,
I'll phone BT and ask them
Please take all phones off the hook.

Constance Vera Dewdney

THE NEIGHBOUR FROM HELL

An environmental vandal
Lives next door, but one -
He lights his stinky bonfires
When my washing's clean and spun
No sooner have I pegged
This and that up on the line
Than acrid smoke starts billowing
Engulfing me and mine
He's been asked nicely not to do this
But he didn't mend his ways
I can't think what he finds to burn -
Though I've not seen his wife for days!

Anne Polhill Walton

A RAGING NATION

We are a nation
of frustration
We stand in line
and then we whine
We wave our fists
and curse and swear
We now have road rage
everywhere
There's now a rage
of every kind
Which we accept
don't seem to mind

Why don't we all
once in a while
Stand back, deep breath
and give a smile
We make mistakes
but not to worry
We can always say
we're sorry

If someone else
looks for a fight
Just smile and say
'You must be right'
And watch them wince
and then to flounder
As on your peaceful
way you wander

Let's be a nation
not of frustration
We can be one
that's full of fun
Let us conjoin
in harmony
Why don't we start
with you and me?

Donald L Carey

MORONS - BELT UP

There are still many of them, wherever you go
And it's not as if they're driving extremely slow
It is the Mums and Dads that make me so cross
And in the end it is going to be their loss!
They let their kids sit on someone's lap in the front
Don't they know the child will get the force of the brunt
They leave them to hang out of open windows to laugh
A close passing vehicle could end a real blood bath
Toddlers are seen in the back standing up to look
Wouldn't it be safer, them strapped in, with a book
Seat belts to be put in the back - can be a cost
But not nearly as dear as a child that is lost
New cars already have these fitted in the rear
As experts have already seen and had this fear
All out there who have little ones, with you I plead
Do not let it be your neglect that makes them bleed
They are bought into the world to be loved by you
Don't let it be your stupidity that kills them too!

Penny Brown

Litter Bug

Deposiphobia is the name
Of an illness shared by hordes,
Who seem to find it quite a game
To ignore *No Litter* boards.
Boxes made of wood or wire,
Stone or metal, are no good -
None can light the inner fire
To put their garbage where they should.
Braced against the litter bin
The sufferer will take aim,
And with an admirable spin
New scattering record claim.
Keep Tidy signs seem to goad
This wretched feckless bunch,
Who strew along the public road
The wrappings from their lunch . . .
If packaging would all degrade,
I would not be so bitter,
As in each public place I wade
Through someone else's litter.

Di Bagshawe

No, I'm Not Interested In Babies!

No
I'm not interested in babies
And no
I haven't got a boyfriend
No
I'm not wanted to get married
And no
I don't want a house of my own.
No
I can't afford a car
(I hate driving anyway)
No I don't go drinking
And clubbing I can't stand.

Yes!
I'm different!
Why can't people see
I'm not of their mould
And have no wish to be.

Is it wrong
To conceive the future
As the next choreographical idea?
Why not map the months ahead
With 'what shall I write now'?

My horizons
Are widely open.
I'm looking forward
To my Eternal Destiny!

Anna Kemble

FREEDOM OF SPEECH

Although I am a woman, from the city born and bred,
I love Mother Nature, it really has to be said.
I know buildings have to be built, on this beautiful land,
for people to live in, bricks, mortar and sand.
I for one know that progress has to be made,
but for the sake of our grandchildren, I feel so afraid.
Please don't cut down all the trees, flowers and green,
for in the end, nothing but concrete jungles to be seen!
No branches for the blackbird to sit, and dedicate his beautiful song,
on a warm balmy summer's evening, never again will he belong.
To walk through a carpet of bluebells, in the woodlands and dell,
in God's wondrous countryside is my Heaven, *not* a treeless Hell!

Christine Anne Thurling

War

Bang, bang go the guns.
Sound of death upon the cliffs.
While I - I sit and gaze out
over a scene of unparalleled beauty.
So peaceful here -
water lapping, seagulls crying and sun shining.
But all the time behind are the noises of execution.
Sun gleams on shimmering water,
reflecting jewelled turquoise of the sky.
All here is perfect in its peace,
peaceful, still and yet -
as violent as the rape of purity,
are the noises which disturb.
Noise so brutal and harsh.
A game, a practice they say and yet
grim reminder, dark foreboding
of the evil reality of man,
the supreme power of destruction, held within our hands.
Power come to us through ancient evil,
fed and strengthened down the years.
Through this power life is twisted,
where, to protect their lives, people would destroy life.
And man would stretch out a hand
to kill, sooner than a heart to love.
All around is the beauty of our land and world,
yet man cannot see or understand -
locked in the search for destruction.
And the sounds of death are all around.

Anne Tompsett

WASTE

'Think of the starving millions,' my mother would berate,
If feeling full at mealtimes, I left food on my plate,
Here in the cafeteria if she could only see,
The waste disposal unit guzzles more than me,
The mounds of sweets and savouries abandoned by the greedy,
Are half-devoured, so would not serve to feed the poor and needy,
Tomato ketchup covered chips lie scattered all around,
Like dead and dying soldiers on some war torn battle ground,
Compost heaps of pasties adorned with squashy peas,
Keep company with jacket spuds denuded of their cheese,
Congealed across the tables, lakes of curry sauce and beans,
Create a gallery of pictures of amazing abstract scenes,
Fleets of shipwrecked doughnuts becalmed on plastic trays,
Tempt colonies of buzzing wasps to feed upon their glaze,
Half-full cups of fizzy drinks, like rainbow coloured seas,
Discarded now, they just provide a watery grave for bees,
This wanton waste just goes to show there's money to be spent,
Not only on the water, electricity and rent,
Most people order meals as if they're going out of fashion,
Gorging 'til they're fit to burst with animal-like passion,
They may leave the scene, but mounds of leftovers remain,
And some time later back they come, and off they scoff again,
But worse than this, is all the food that goes a different route,
Those unsold cakes and pasties that end up down the chute,
If we all experienced real hunger, perhaps we'd understand,
And value nature's bounties in this green and fertile land.

Katy Melia

TWENTIETH CENTURY

Inventions and discoveries, remarkable feats
Social injustice, riots on our streets
Space exploration who would have guessed
Footsteps on the moon, an unimaginable quest
Two world wars and millions oppressed
Third world problems still to be addressed
Medical advances bringing cures for many diseases
Technological developments, the wonder never ceases
Yet with these achievements comes a price to pay
Inequality amongst the masses and inner-city decay
Global uprisings against corruption and greed
Military dictatorships plant a fruitless seed
The population boom means more mouths to feed
Opportunities dependant upon colour and creed
Money and power become targets of the rich
The cry of the poor becomes 'life's a bitch'
As the end of the century approaches, does the candle still glow
For a brighter future, only time will show

Ewan Walker

FORGIVENESS?

'I remember when this was fields and trees,' an old man said to me
'multi-shaded greenery as far as you could see
but now there's bricks and mortar in every corner spare
they're creating hideous landscapes and they just don't seem to care.'

What used to be a pasture green where farmers reared their flocks
is now a close or housing park with homes all built on plots
with ponds and flowers in the back and neat lawns at the front
it's stolen land from long ago where wildlife used to hunt.

They say there's too much traffic and we need another road
so they cut down trees and plough through fields
no care for bird or toad
and they do not care for the brooks and streams
and do not see the meadow
with the cows and horses roaming around in a sea of buttercup yellow.

Why does no one realise the damage they're creating
the men in suits don't care for us nor for the land they're taking
they care not for the future they think only today
they do not think of children or where they all might play.

And what about the future? There'll soon be nothing left
but tarmac, bricks, cement and glass, we should be charged with theft
so let's for once forget ourselves, forget our fancy living
and maybe in the time to come we may just be forgiven!

Steve Hughes

FAMINE

Eyes stare blankly into space
Piercing eyes from a sad little face
Eyes that show the world their pain
Eyes that search and pray for rain

A sea of people follow a trail
Young and old so weak and frail
No child should have to suffer such pain
Why do their lives seem so in vain?

For some the help is there to find
From people who are caring, gentle and kind
For some the help is found too late
They lie forsaken, doomed to their fate!

The rest of the world argue and fight
About things they want to put to right
Instead we all should love and give,
Give these children the right to live!

K A Coleran

FREE FOR ALL

It is wonderful to be free
And to live in the land of my birth
Surely this must be the greatest joy on earth
And yet for all this cannot be
There are some that are ruled by bureaucracy
Others are ruled by sheer corruption
And their countries are on the edge of destruction
Little children who only reach knee high
Are battered and bruised and left to die
Some are made to work like the ox
By people more cunning than the fox
And when others try to ease their plight
They are shot at, beaten and put to flight
Why can't people be happy with what they need
What turns need into voracious greed
Let's turn, again to the pioneer spirit
Let's cleanse the world of the rot that's in it
Then each man, woman and little child
Can walk this earth with joy and pride
There will be no place for hypocrisy
Only freedom peace and democracy

Jean Kennedy

IN OUR OWN WORLDS

Communications grow faster,
Reaching, linking, crawling into our lives.
And yet,
We're lonely.

In our own worlds,
We sit silent,
Absorbing,
But seldom really talking.

Intimacy? Expression?
Communication slowly renders us mute.

Katrina Payne

AND SO I KNOCK

The door is locked and so I knock,
        but no-one answers.
Has God gone out, or does He peep
        to see who's knocking there?
Is He inside and wants to hide
        from those who ask for help?
Is He tired of what He sees
        and is distressed, upon His knees?
I stand and pray for strength
        to keep me sane.

What happened to the time
        when we could visit there.
To be refreshed and filled with loving care.
To kneel and feel the caring hand upon our shoulder
        and know that someone shared our heavy load.
Must we accept that some
        don't fear,
        do not respect,
        cannot control their greed,
        and so His house is locked.

But don't stand knocking.
'Look,' I hear Him say,
        'at the beauty of the flowers
        and you will see Me there.
Listen to the song of the birds
        and the flowing stream
        and hear My music.
Feel the gentle breeze.'
        Don't doubt the presence of God,
        His power is all around.

Dorothy Fisher

O DIANA!

Many, many the flowers laid upon the ground.
Many, so many more the tears of the people,
Passionately sad, caught in the act of living,
Crossed in confrontation with the violent death of
An unhappy heroine, so deeply flawed. Drowned,
The day's hypocrisy. From a muffled steeple
Tolls a shame openly in honour of giving
Without taking as, for a moment, the breath of
Love's silence overcomes the teeming city's sound.
Shrilly her song speaks and unites all our feeble
Effort within her coffin . . . disfigured . . . striving
Hopelessly 'gainst every private hell and heaven.

6 September 1997

William Basil McLaughlin

FREEDOM

The freedom to escape,
From chains that bond the heart.
The freedom to feel joy
And from misery to depart.

The freedom of the chosen words,
To fall without the blame.
The freedom to teach of love
And in your heart feel others' shame.

The freedom to console the sick,
The poor, deprived and needy.
The freedom to feel pity,
For the cruel, destructive and greedy.

The freedom to fight for justice and right,
Without recrimination.
The freedom of help from a fellow man,
Without fear of obligation.

The freedom to be surrounded,
By those we know and love.
The freedom to wish for peace,
Whose emblem is the dove.

The freedom to tread safely,
Knowing danger is not near.
The freedom of every soul alive,
To live life without fear.

Jan Trivett

Proud OAPs

We're OAPs but don't be fooled
Our staying power just won't be ruled,
So do not look at us and jeer
We were the ones who got a cheer,
Back in nineteen forty four
With Hitler knocking at our door,
We were the ones that paved the way
For all you young ones here today,
You may think you had it rough
But rest assured our lives were tough,
Food was scarce, money too
Sometimes we didn't know what to do,
To make 'ends meet' was quite a task
Our pride refused to let us ask
For help and hand-outs like today,
We tried to manage on our pay,
Which was quite small compared to now
But cope we did - I don't know how,
If this sounds boring let me say
We're strong as ever - come what may,
And when our pensions we collect
With our head held high,
It's because we earned it
From the years gone by,
So do not look at us and jeer
We were the ones that got you here.

Patricia Battye

ABATTOIR

Sing they when slaughtering,
My kisses were for you,
In which snails sleep . . .
It could have been you,
But . . .
Would the beautiful take it?
Bungalow, do the takes . . .
With, the ice-cream man, so . . .
Don't caramel without me,
Scholars in circle studded skies,
A needle in the park,
Long hair in the dark,
Go to work on an egg.

Tracie Mark Deakin

PERISH THE THOUGHT

Give them to murderers
Men who rape,
But for God's sake
Don't give them to two women
Who love each other.

Perish the thought.
I mean what kind of mothers would they make?
Surely the child would not be straight!
But straight are their parents,
(You seem to forget).

It's alright to give them
To fathers who love
(A little too much).

Or subject them to a loveless couple.
Who think a child
Would make everything fine.

Just because they love other women
Doesn't make the feelings less strong.
Mother Nature intended them to have children,
Whether it be right or wrong.

Would you rather them stuff up their lives?
Because they think nobody cares,
Or feel needed and wanted
By a committed, loving pair,
Of dykes.

Amanda Allbones

MAELSTROM

I lay me on my couch awhile
To ponder on man's present ills
I fell into a dreaming state
Far from the maelstrom men create.
From turmoil, crimes and roving bands
Of terrorists in many lands,

From greed and cheating everywhere -
For honest folk it's hard to bear.
But sands of time are running low
For those whose lust and greed bestow

On this fair earth a growing blight
But profit makes these things alright.
Many creatures' homes are taken
Faith in God is being shaken,

But faith in God should not be blamed
For human values that have changed.
And so, for this short space I dream
Of far, untravelled shores, so clean

Where all God's creatures, homes can find
And leave this mad turmoil behind.
But needs I must back to my couch,
And waken to the clangerous march

Of stressful news as it arrives,
The changing to redundant lives.
Affairs of humans now gone mad
Change this, change that, it's very sad.

Where it should be co-operative,
Instead, compete - creating hate.
No time, no time it seems, to care
No more the time to stand and stare.

G Richardson

LAND OF THE FREE

People here often sneer
about government and bureaucracy.
They should be glad they live in England
Land of freedom and democracy.
When mocking they should stop
and think how different life would be
if every anti establishment joke they crack
earned the wrath of political hierarchy.

The press, TV and the BBC
enjoy freedom unknown in war torn zones
They denounce, scorn and sneer at
all we hold dear.
Writing satires, they're sure
there'll be no knock on the door
heralding arrest for what they do best -
holding up to scorn
the land where they were born.
No need to secrete savage words on microfiche
How lucky for them we have freedom of speech.

Sheila Jones

DUNBLANE

The Queen went to open a museum in Leeds
To glorify guns which 'give rise to great deeds'.
She compared them to music and poetry fine
And talked about craftsmanship, art and design.
But two days before, in a school in Dunblane
A town was beginning a lifetime of pain
And innocent children were shot in the head.
A gymnasium littered with dying and dead.
But, parents, take comfort if you've lost your sons
At the hands of a lunatic bristling with guns.
The weapons were probably great works of art
And the finest of craftsmen blew your lives apart.

Joan Packham

ALIENS

Sir, you're right, our greatest enemy
Are the Humans on planet Earth
And I too look forward to the day
Of that very last Human birth.

And yes, there's a danger they'll expand
Colonise surrounding space
Introducing wars and pollution
To every Milky-Way race.

But, I am absolutely certain
That this council will all agree
Those war-loving money-mad Humans
Are their own worst enemy.

For years we've observed them from afar
As one war ends, another begins
And although many millions die in agony
Nothing changes whoever wins.

So, there's no need for us to talk
Of things like armed confrontation
Because their *politicians* will bring the demise
Of that gullible Human nation.

I have a theory, okay, sounds incredible
But the more I study the Human race
The more I'm convinced their politicians
Are Aliens from outer space.

These Aliens, posing as politicians
Brainwash Humans to put gold before bread
Create wars, diseases, pollution
Till one day . . . all Humans will be dead.

Billy Kennedy

MR PRESIDENT

Dear Mr President,
Stop the continuation of star-wars
Bring down all the satellites
And space stations sent
Into the stratosphere.
Do not destroy our atmosphere.
Tomorrow may be too late
To save my grandchild's future
I entreat you to reconsider
Call a halt, set a date.
Colossal global warming
Is our last fateful warning
Consider, alter, relent
No more emissions destroying
No more missiles deploying
Allow the unborn of our morrow
A life to enjoy and live and follow -
Please, Mr President.

Patricia McDonald

CONSOLATION

We know no words of comfort
        To ease the pain within
And to say we are sorry
        Seems such a little thing
And yet we know as mothers
        How great the loss you bear
United by your sorrow
        We remember you in prayer
God give you consolation
        As greet each darkened morn
Little children oft times die
        As angels they're reborn
So through your heartache and your
        Pain may some joy be known
In the knowledge that your tiny angel
        May be administering at his throne
And there for you their interceding
        So you must dry your tears for
Heaven's for eternity, Earth is measured
        Just by years.

Teresa Dyas

PARKINSON'S
(Ivan started with Parkinson's in September 1993)

I look at my husband many times a day
There's a lump in my throat I am sorry to say
He'd retired from work and six months went by
An illness struck him, I wanted to cry.
His hand started to shake, his foot did the same
You wonder what it is - well Parkinson's the name.
An acupuncturist was tried with his doctor's consent
To slow Parkinson's down, this treatment was meant.
Needles were placed in his hand, foot and head
He'd go to sleep as he laid on the bed.
For two whole years, his treatment he had
But Parkinson's took over, he became worse and I was sad
He went to the Queen's hospital to a neurologist there
To be a patient under his care
He was given tablets and the dosage increased
He'll never be free of Parkinson's, this horrible beast
For 46 years I've had my band of gold
46 years 'to have and to hold',
I hope and pray to God above
We have many years together to offer my love.

Sheila Barker

CHUNNEL VISION!

I liked pounds, shillings and pence
And roast beef on Sunday served at one.
I like warm jam scones and drinking tea with milk
In an English country garden with roses round the lawn.

I never wanted to join other continents
And all become part of a great big whole
I don't want a 'Euro' for the money in my purse
When part of the fun is in the exchange.

I never wanted a channel tunnel
Burrowing deep under the sea
With one side using meters and the other using feet
I wondered; 'Maybe in the middle - they'll miss?'

I wanted to go on measuring knitting in inches
And ordering milk not by litres, but pints.
I want to eat cornflakes and toast for my breakfast
And stay dress size ten - not E48!

I wanted our race to stay as an island
Pleasantly surrounded by the sea.
When 'Going Abroad' meant catching a ferry
Or at least a plane journey over the sea!

Please don't accuse me of being 'Anti'
Of disliking Spaniards or French or the Dutch
I don't have a problem with other nations
I love to go travelling - from my island home.

Call me old fashioned if you name me at all
But I find my solace in not feeling alone
When I state from my heart that I wanted to stay -
Eccentrically - absolutely - quintessentially English!

Sue Ashdown

LIKE TO LIKE ONLY
(For the chimpanzees 'retired' from space research and given for medical experiments)

They shall not 'go gentle into that good night',
Which spreads from star to star,
Who travel on tortured creatures' backs,
Other than what we are.

And even when their travail's done
And apes retire from toil,
Still they serve Man with their bodies
And cannot escape the coil.

'Given', they are, for experiments
To ease the bones of Man
And broken, their own, in a cause not theirs
That only a few seek to ban.

What will star races say of us
Who use our cousins so?
And will they wish to know us then
Or, in horror, tell us, 'Go!'?

From world to world to wander
With only those to call us friend
Who likewise torture animals
When to the stars they send.

I H Pyves

WINNING THE NATIONAL LOTTERY

Oh for a win on the lottery
All our problems will be solved,
We would go on foreign holidays
And see what else could be evolved.

Oh for a win on the lottery
To buy that brand new car,
We could show it off to all our friends
And drive it far and far.

Oh for a win on the lottery
To buy up all those sites,
To clean them up and redevelop,
And fit them all with neon lights.

Oh for a win on the lottery
For a place down by the sea,
Where we could go and swim all day
And not come home till tea.

Oh for a win on the lottery
To invest in all those shares,
We'd be rich, we'd be rich,
And could throw away our cares.

Oh for a win on the lottery
To live in the grandest style,
With mansion, servants, lakes and garden
Getting pampered all the while.

Oh, we won the National Lottery
And what did we achieve?
Begging letters and financial advisers
And not what you believe -
Happiness!

Nicholas Freville

FAME

Fickle fingers of fame touch my eager receptors -
Taunt and tease torn ego.
Has fame touched you?
Are you left feeling bereaved bereft of breath?
Or are you still mesmerised in a moving mist and trance?
Are you dancing moving to the irrepressible tortuous tunes
Of Astaire and Rogers Harlow and Handel Monroe and Milligan.
'Hold! Don't move! Shoot!
No dearie - not you!'
You're just another Extra to join the queue
Of Media Cannon-fodder - surplus to requirements
Of other more famous Stars.
Your voice won't be selling HP sauce or Oxo cubes . . .
But wait a minute aren't you already selling something
Much more important?
Write your own lyrics sing your own song?
Play with words to make the whole world sing and dance
In one long chant of Truth
Reach the parts other well worn words have made
And feed the sensibility anew in fresh fields of dew.
Who needs to fan the flames of fickle fame past its sell-by date . . .
We're all famous without public applause of the Mass
True value for money! Aren't we!

Paula Fox

I Wonder Why

I wonder why the council could be so lax
Making me pay such a lot of tax!
There is no doubt, I am disappointed,
They have left me feeling, rather daunted!

No place to park my car
Pavements widened far too far
Police station's early closed
While, I pay thro' the nose!

Children have nowhere to go
Parks are only made for show!
Hanging baskets, fountain, flower beds
No wonder I'm in the red!

Television camera, viewing the streets
It's enough to make one weep
I'll just end with a sigh
I - wonder why?

Maisie Roberts

The Wall

For years, it goaded his idealism.
For years, it affronted his humanity,
circumscribed his sense of community.

For years, therefore, he tried to destroy it.
Sometimes, impatient of restraint, he went for it,
tried direct assault, tried going under or over.

Dreaming of mountains, though, best enabled him
to transcend it, prompted his best work.
Nevertheless, in moments of despair, he was moved

to daub insults upon it. Finally, however,
when all hope seemed to have gone,
finally, one day, like a dinosaur whose moment

of extinction has come - it just collapsed!
Giving access to a limitless, labour-saved, community of choice,
with horizons pre-cooked, pre-canned, pre-packaged;

bulk-bought, deep frozen, marked-down, on offer -
a prospect that looked so unexpectedly flat,
he felt like defecating on an abundance so spotless.

But, instead, responding to the new challenge,
painstakingly - and in defiance of all outrage,
of all defacement, of all accusations of decadence

which anyway, in the end, gave way to widespread
indifference - painstakingly, on a cordon of canvas,
he painted cans - in the image of mountains.

Kevin Worsnop

A Literary Article

I, here and now, present my case.
I find it is a sheer disgrace,
The load of litter that accrues
Along the streets and avenues,
For, when I'm on my morning run,
I find I get more fret than fun,
For rubbish, left by Jack and Jill,
Fill every prospect with ill will.
Now, once, I grabbed a litter lout,
To teach him what it's all about,
But, as he was just four foot five,
I jibbed at skinning him alive,
But, his response to my complaint,
Would try the patience of a saint,
And, as for me, it's well known that
Forbearance isn't what I'm at,
But even I would never quote
The threats that issued from his throat.
(Such shocking sinful words of spite
The Moving Finger wouldn't write).
Those were the days, when life was good,
And discipline was understood,
And toys, now on the rubbish cart,
Were cherished till they fell apart.

G E M Broomhead

LEGALISED ROBBERY

Been away so long, hell it's a mess
The disappearance of my old address
Another terrace row comes crashing down
Changing the face of my home town
Planners and councillors do you really care?
Have you any feelings you and your friends up there?
But the planners are blind as the blind can be
They would sooner have concrete where the grass should be
They stretch us on the rack of bureaucracy
Say we should be humble for the taxes they bleed
It's legalised robbery

The case they make is usually fraudulent
Your money they say is very well spent
Spent wining and dining their favourite contractors
Or on expenses paid trips, long and protracted
Then it's compulsory purchase
We'll give you half price
Then stick you in a tower block, ain't that nice
The children they cry
There's nowhere to play
The planners assassinated another community today
Whilst fat back-handers fill the councillors with glee
The system's just legalised robbery.

Carey Whitehead

FREEDOM OF SPEECH

Dear Hong Kong, I send you this letter
To thank you for all you have done
To let us experience living
In the land of the noonday gun.
We worked hard and played hard and loved it,
The wining and dining and fun
In this place where the world is your oyster
And the food that is second to none.
Now back in the comfort of Britain,
Here in the land of our birth,
Where the cherry trees bloom in the springtime,
And we know what democracy's worth,
We watched as the horror unfolded
And wept with a helpless despair
As the blood and the anguish exploded
And spilled on Tiananmen Square!
Oh, those sweet, gentle almond eyed faces
With all of their futures to give
To the homeland, whose leaders decided
Those students had no right to live!

All they wanted was freedom
To speak and to think and express.
But all they received was the carnage
And a life of unrivalled distress.
Dear Hong Kong, these now are your leaders
And we watch as your future's unfurled
And pray that 'one country, two systems'
Remains for the eyes of the world.

Esma Wilson Wright

NOW THAT'S FOR ME!

I don't like your cities,
Nor your sprawling new towns -
It's not for me.
I don't like your concrete trees,
Your tarmac rivers, steel streams -
No, they're not for me.
Your city pubs and clubs
Mean absolutely nought to me -
No, not to me.
The punch-ups on a Friday night
With young men howling scenting blood -
No, it's not for me.

Give me fields of emerald green
Wide blue sky up above -
Now that's for me!
Cool blue waters running past
Chuckling o'er my feet -
Yes, that's for me!
Friday nights when harvest's home
Devoted to swapping tales of yore -
Yes, now that's for me!
So keep your cities and your towns,
Give me hills and give me streams -
That's for me!

J E Alban

UNBOWED

Jaundiced 'leaders' give the word,
Soul-less 'soldiers' act.
Obscene horrors felt, and heard -
Pyromaniacs tact!
Broken bodies, shattered dreams,
Butchered at a stroke.
And yet, the hope for peace still gleams -
Even through pain's yoke!
Voiceless, agonising pain,
All-consuming grief,
Jangles nerves, and makes the strain
Goad them from belief.
Buried now, their kith and kin,
'Judgement' passed on each.
All victims of the 'killers' sin',
Martyrs of free speech!
Murdered on a summer's day,
So a 'point' is made.
Lost, because of some word-play
Rank politicians brayed!
Frail now, is the 'peace process',
Everybody knows.
Guardedly, you seek progress,
Albeit rather slow.
Future generations *will*
Build on what you do,
Overcoming all that still
Dictate what is true!

M Kennedy

FREEDOM OF SPEECH

To be told as a child to be quiet, in most cases told to shut up,
Shut your mouth or, be silent, and please don't interrupt
Is to deny a child the freedom of speech,
These are not lessons we should teach.
Knowledge is gained, sifted and framed, it is everywhere to find,
That everlasting question, why? Shows an enquiring mind.
Freedom of speech is a right for all, denied in some countries we hear,
One takes a risk to criticise then live day by day in fear.
It is bad for a press to be hampered, to suppress the written word,
Then TV and radio propaganda is all that is ever heard.
People have died for freedom of speech, democracy will prevail,
Truth will stand wherever found, dictatorship will fail.
Examples there are in history show us all we need to know,
People's voices silenced, resentment, revenge, then starts to grow
Into wars, sometimes world-wide, the persecuted run and hide.
Freedom to speak one's mind is all, that causes despots to fail and fall.

Patricia Evans

UNTITLED

They took away my livelihood
Said youths' song must be sung
They took away security
And left dark days to come

They took away belief in truth
In justice and in law
They left behind a bitterness
I'd never felt before

They took away my sense of pride
To feel a job well done
My right to make provision
Was taken for the young

I'm left with deep resentment
That never should have been
Retirement now a nightmare
Surplanter of a dream

Mary Weber

HYDE PARK, LONDON 300 MILES

Lord Bragg, David Maclean,
Lord Steel not far behind.
Leading the march at
The Lowther Horse Trials
Upholding the rights of the countryside
They were there to add weight
To the matter in hand
Their political differences set to one side.
Hunting, fishing, farming and leisure
Everything that spells country marching together.
The crocodile grew as the supporters joined in
The young and the old and the in betweens.
With sure and steady footsteps they marched along
To the strains and the singing of George Bowyer's song.
The voice of the countryside
The Guardians of the land
All making sense to the thousands at hand.
God gave us free will to do what we think is right
But before laws are made, let the powers that be,
Consider long and hard, the ways of the man of the
British countryside.

Helen Wood

MEMORIALS

Remember those who died in vain,
Flowers of an English rain.

Brittle brothers crushed in mud,
In their hearts the dying thud;

Acrid air no more to breathe
Under the blackened, blasted tree.

So many bodies upward stare
As its great root, the hidden share;

A bitter harvest from the grain
That seeded crosses on the plain;

And withered sages grimly nod -
They got it wrong. Now sleep with God.

Graeme Vine

THE EARTH'S CRY

The world is getting destroyed,
Oh what can I do?
Spin around helplessly,
While knowing that those rampaging adults are destroying the Earth
That they live in. It's the younger generation, *your* generation, that
Will suffer in the future to come.

What can I do, but just sit here in the
Middle of space and dream of a better life . . .
A life where all the air is pollutant free and
The birds fly in harmony,
Where the grass in the meadows is green,
And the forests and trees survive till a thousand years,
Where all animals live in their own habitat.
Where a world has all the seasons bright and gay, where the animals
Come and go their way.
A life where, where . . .

Oh, forget it! What am I thinking of? Snap back to the real world.
What world? I'm the world that's getting destroyed.
All the natural resources are being ripped of their roots.
Stop burning all that 'fossil fuel'! Can't you see we're starting to live
In a 'greenhouse' with increasing acid rain. All the beautiful trees,
Fishes and buildings are being stripped, killed and crumpled down to
The ground.
Stop building nuclear power stations! One of the main problems is how
To get rid of it all?
Why cut down the forests? Without the forests you Earthlings won't be
Able to breath. You have no life without trees.
Think about it. Even you can do something about the Earth's future by
Cutting down pollution and saving the Earth's riches, which are close to
Extinction.
Remember, it's *your* future. Do something about it!

Thuha Auda

OMAGH

28 too many people died that Saturday,
how can they ask for independence in this bloody way?

Simple intelligence fails to understand,
the bloodlust that may lie in the heart of a man.

And who can give the answers to those who pray?
But awoke to find their lives torn away.

Innocent people sharing peaceful beliefs,
they were just out shopping on their local streets.

The worst atrocity of them all,
is that these poor people were led to their fall.

A whole generation has been brought up in fear,
their only hope now is that the end must be near.

Janine Ellis

IS GOD DIRECTING EARTHLY LIFE AS A THEATRICAL PLAY?

The stage is the vast land and sea
forming planet earth,
human beings currently play the leading role,
plants and animals complete the cast,
whose emotional drive is love in their soul,
the soundtrack is all music of present and past,
the plot is to keep planet earth moving -
is God directing earthly life
as a theatrical play?

When analysing our actions and reactions,
our reasons for behaving so,
in the light of the omnipotent universe,
they pale into a tiny shadow,
of meaningless conflicts,
posing more questions than giving answers.

Are our minds programmed by God,
or are our minds independent?
Do we hold a greater universal meaning,
or are we here to entertain our creator?

With every decade that sets the scenes,
we seem like faking more in our lives,
ignoring the truth, seeing no meaning why,
acting a brief part in a play no one survives,
we perform carelessly like screaming goodbye
with our desperate voice -
is there another place the human race arrives,
or don't we have any choice,
but to face our extermination day?

Is God directing earthly life
as a theatrical play?

Rune Brokstad

IF THE ANTI'S GET THEIR WISH

I walk along the river bank,
Where I spent so many days.
Memories come flooding back
All in a golden haze.
Memories are all I have,
For no longer can I fish.
Those bloody anti anglers,
Have finally got their wish.

If they changed the law tomorrow,
It would still be far too late.
There are no fish here any more,
They've already met their fate.
They were poisoned months ago,
The river is now dead.
Where once the anglers could be seen,
There's piles of junk instead.

And what of all the anti's?
Do they ever come to see?
What their victory got them
Do they walk the bank like me?
No they never come here,
They have no interest now.
There is no peaceful fisherman,
With which to start a row.

When the anglers left the rivers,
There was no one to care.
No one who loved the rivers.
Just for being there.
The anti's and polluters,
Both must share the blame.
For turning all our rivers,
Into lifeless drains.

So I walk along the river bank,
Where I used to fish.
And hope that they are satisfied,
Now the anti's have got their wish.

G Hollinsworth

MINES

Did he think?
Did he care?
As he laid the *mine* . . .
Hidden by the grasslands.

Would he look back?
Wondering?
How will it be . . .
The *explosion!*

Is *he* alive?
Does he see, does he hear?
Torn limbs . . .
Death.

Is he ashamed?
What does *he* feel?
Will we ever know or . . .
Conceive this carnage of innocent victims.

Joan M Hopkins

Power Of Speech

To have the power of speech and say
The things that's in our hearts
It's all the hatred in this world
That's tearing it apart
If everyone could see some good
In a person that has none
I'm sure that the spoken word
Is better than a gun
But people get angry from time to time
And cannot see the truth
For if love shows itself, they are fine
Then they seem to block it out
And instant of a friendly smile
They just stand and shout
And then the hatred shows itself
And love is out of reach
Then you find they use the gun
Instead of the power of speech.

Joyce E Williams

Democracy

We moan about this country
Of taxes rates and such
We moan about our leaders
And say they're out of touch
But we are very lucky
That we can voice our thoughts
Without looking o'er our shoulders
In fear, lest we be caught
We do not know the horror
We do not know the dread
Of being thrown in prison
For something that we've said
Our children go for schooling
It's absolutely free
As is their health and welfare
I think you would agree -
No government is perfect
No government is great
But I for one am thankful
That we have our Welfare State.

Dianne J Shorthouse

GHOST THE BOMB

'When we ghost the shadow of the bomb.'
Then we'll know: That 'love' has overcome:

There's far too much in the larder; there's too much in the home;
Too much accent on, 'the good life', when the other half have none:
Too much waste! Too much profit! While they bicker over billions:
'Shouldn't we think about the sick? The homeless in their millions?'
'They're right here in our midst; if only we can see them.'
'There's more than enough for everyone if only it was even:-'
'They're oh! so near; yet oh! so far - but just across the sea;
'I'm sure we can reach them - if we use our ability;'
'Remember! Our Cambodia; embracing all her sons -'
With reverence at 'Christmas', and: every day that comes.

Selina Styles

Our Fireman

When people think of uniform
They think 'the boys in blue'
But don't forget the fireman
For they wear blue, too

When they hear a siren
Or see him on his beat
They don't think of the fireman
Working in the heat

They see the uniform as law and order
But haven't got a clue
How hard the fireman has to train
And all they really do

A lot think that a fireman
Has lots of time to play
They just think they fool around
And play snooker all the day

They think they put out fires
Until no more embers glow
They don't think about the accidents
To which they have to go

They see a cat stuck up a tree
Brought down by scruff of neck
They don't see the little children
Cut out from a wreck

But if you ask the fireman
Take heed of his replies
They'll tell a different story
To open up your eyes

The fireman sees those children
Has to take it in his stride
He works till sweat runs down his back
And does his job with pride

He sees the thick black smoke
And the flames all red
He sees the charred up buildings
And he sees the dead

He sees the ones that fall asleep
Forgetting they are smoking
He carries them to safety
And tries to stop them choking

So all you people with your doubts
And nowt to shout about
Remember when you're in trouble
The fireman gets you out

So people change your attitude
Show respect just now and then
They're not just some more boys in blue
They're heroes, our firemen.

B D Grindy

BENEFIT OF CLERGY

'Radix malorum est cupiditas -
The root of evils is the love of brass:'
    The Pardoner's text was ever thus.
'Shun avarice, lest you be dragged to hell.
Give freely, be absolved, I'll see you well.'
    Much cash he counted in his cell . . .

Thus people paid for paradise to come.
Were any disappointed? - they were dumb.
    A beautiful protection scam!
But still the punters pay and priests collect:
Do they deliver? - or deserve respect?
    Perhaps if they declined all cheques . . .

John Hatton Davidson

TO THE ABUSER

I wear my mask most every day
at work, at home and at play
a mask to make the world seem fair
when I am drowning in despair.

Despair at things that I have known
that have not left as I have grown
things I keep locked in my mind
that no one knows and cannot find.

A guilty weight that I have borne
of a shattered childhood I know mourn
an innocence brought to a premature end
and wounds that now can never mend

I cannot sleep at all, can you?
then destroying lives is what you do
I hope you read this now it's done
and see the cost of your surreptitious fun.

Eilidh McMillan

DOES ANYBODY CARE?

The days when children played in the streets
Have not gone;
Only the days when it used to be safe.

A Humphrey

NOT HONEST ANYMORE

People not honest anymore
No longer honest with themselves
Not like in the war
Indeed!
Which war was that?
People tell themselves
Not listen anymore
That this and that is right
That so and so is good
Indeed!
But where does right come from?
Where does the good thing live?
People not happy anymore
Strangers from another place
A different race
Indeed!
Devoid of grace
A bit like us
That's all
People not honest anymore

Dave Pearson

WHY?

The bomb has now dropped
The silence of screams,
That place, once of beauty
No longer serene.
Search through the rubble
With some hope, and a prayer,
But where are your family?
Don't give up, they've got to be there.
Then that necklace you see
Belonging from old,
The nightmare has come
Truth begins to unfold.
You're not the only one
The whole town's in despair,
You scream, shout and cry
Why's life so unfair?
Babies and children, maimed
Before their life has begun,
Why's it so tragic?
Life's meant to be fun.
What have they done
To make them suffer such pain?
Just innocent victims
Of our world, gone insane.
Whatever country it is
That you come from,
We all suffer the same
When someone drops that bomb.
Man's not man's enemy, it's weapons and war,
They destroy everyone's life, and what was it for?

Susan Evelyn Churton

THE PRECINCT

Enter all -
my magic doors entice you in
my pristine halls
await your exploration
step slowly to your fix
but mind -
my pretty floors
designed for dawdlers
are, of course too slippery
for hurrying feet

Step inside my floodlit caves
feel free to browse
try one of these
or these or these
see my goodies all arranged
in buy me, buy me
colourful displays

An hour or two of perfect world
of instant access plastic cash
unlimited availability
try one of these or these or these
a boost for the economy
(but only during daylight hours -
and drunks and dogs and cigarettes
are not allowed)

Don't stop to wonder at the waste
don't spoil your day
don't ask how dear
the guarded, gleaming
artificial atmosphere

Shirley Frost

ANGER

I feel anger, humiliation, and despair
Unbelievable bigotry, from rectors who should care,
Enter the house of the Lord, each may say
Give your hearts to Jesus, for he's there day by day
Find peace in His being
Know He is all knowing and seeing
Forgive . . . those that harm, in so many ways
Put your trust in the Savour, these are his teachings they say.

Then through torment and heartbreak, your life almost ends
Yet the loving hands of a stranger, pulls you round rugged bends
Soon the stars shine even whiter
And dark days seem much brighter
Once more into God's house, to walk side by side
A fifty year old couple, to be husband and bride
But no, no, never, not in their churches, may you wed
Divorced although blameless, do it any other way it is said
Such anger, humiliation, and despair
To be spurned by God's ministers, for in his house to marry there.

Susan Goldsmith

QUEST FOR PEACE

The countryside was crying
All through last night's sleep;
I heard the mountain's discontent
And I could only weep.
The trees which rustled in the day
Caught the settled breeze,
They tried to turn it autumn shades
Captured in the leaves.
Anticipation in the air
For morning's yet to dawn,
Hopeful feelings greet the day
The wish for peace is born.
The moody night watches over
Heavenly intervention
While all the world is waiting for
The calm it will not mention.
No more sorrow, no more pain,
Embracing a new future
The night of apprehension ends
As man unites with nature.

Diane Antoniazzi

EINSTEIN'S PHILADELPHIA

In Germany the war began to threaten Einstein's work,
so he went to America where he would be more free,
to practice his new science in space time if they'd agree.

A place called Philadelphia had a nice Naval Yard,
where the crew of the Eldridge volunteered to work quite hard.

Tried out upon the Eldridge the experiment was to be,
the Unified Field Theory Einstein's work in forty-three.

As generators started magnetic coils threw force,
out to the vessel and her crew who never knew the source.

A magnetic field tremendous was thrown around the ship,
people saw it disappear they thought they'd lost their grip.

It appeared at a dockyard a good few miles away,
the plan had gone just as they wished, science had held its sway.

Until the men came back and were really odd, insane,
they all had nightmares of a void a different spatial plane.

Although it proved to Einstein that there were other times,
the wives whose husbands damaged stayed thought these
things were all crimes.

We never hear of anyone who wants to try it now,
to volunteer for time-travel has become a sacred cow.

Jean Paisley

FAMINE

Millions of people die each day
It doesn't have to be this way.

Famine is not a nice way to die,
To say death is peaceful is just a lie.
Screams for water, pangs of hunger,
The pain they feel is just like torture.

Millions of people die each day,
It doesn't have to be this way.

They know the way life's going to be
I know I'm glad that it's not me.
I hear the sound of children crying,
I look around see parents dying.

Millions of people die each day,
It doesn't have to be this way.

Why should they have to live like this?
Prepared to them, we live in bliss.
Surely shouldn't there be a law,
To stop the famine, once and for all?

Millions of people die each day,
We've got money, why don't we pay?

Sophie Johnson

Legacy

There is silence over the river banks,
dark waters' stagnant frown,
the dead and leaning reeds,
a petrified brown.

No waterfowl make the sounds,
of life living wail,
once where grew green foliage,
now spreads a deathly pale.

All along the water lanes,
built up to concrete view,
no winding greenbelt to wend,
just motor vehicles spew.

Above the skies grow darker,
no birds are seen to fly,
not a sight of their homecoming,
in our indifference, did we hear their cry?

Only monstrous flying ships,
their noise the only sound,
and thunderclouds block out the moon,
as lightning spears the ground.

Seas around the coastline turned to poisoned soup,
fish no longer spawn there, no seabirds left to scoop,
for animals and mammals the humans found no use,
the horizon leaves no invitation, for which to build a dream.
No traveller goes there, for there is no beauty to be seen.

Joan McAvoy

TERRORIST

T hugs in a cesspit of hatred,
E vil corrupting and inbred;
R ats commandeered by the devil,
R abid destructive and cruel.
O ppression and fear is their leaning;
R eligion to them has no meaning.
I nnocents suffer their brutality;
S atan dictates their philosophy;
T raitors of democracy.

Lynda Sumbler

SMILING, YOUNG TONY

There's no finer model than our splendid, most honourable Tony Blair.
Guaranteed to be so active that his trousers' seat abhors the easy chair.
One minute he's in Paris and the next, strolling through Omagh town.
For a busy person, he makes a determined effort, to suss out all around.

The grass won't grow under his feet for he never stays put long enough.
You can see he rates a very high calibre, his mind being sharp
and tough.
On tricky question-time debates you'd deem he'd flounder and flumble.
Never a fear of that for he causes his astute antagonist's ploys
to crumble.

He likes to get to the bottom of things and see whole objectives
through.
He really weeded out Ulster, which was a most daring achievement
to do.
If for nothing else, he'll slot into history books, as a most
determined lad.
He rescued 'The Royals' in their darkest hour, which surely can't
be bad!

Before he came to power there was sore criticism about his
silvery smile.
Many wondered if it were real or just rented from London's
Golden Mile.
Even in the thickest of debates, it suddenly appears and twinkles
so wide.
You can see it's the genuine article which he polishes with
perfect pride.

No matter how you disagree with his politics, you must admire his style!
Never vague, he's spurred Happy Hague, to ramble o'er hills for a while.
He's the darling of a blonde baroness, whose efforts he refused to revile.
Such a remarkable chap, so perfectly pat, he seems just impossible to rile.

T Burke

STOP!

Stop the running victim,
Stop the chasing party;
We ask you:
Does cruelty really suggest to you some sort of a sport?
Innocent creatures chased to their death
Of shredding and ripping at the flesh.
Does that give you something to enjoy, something to look forward to?
Maybe for you . . .
But put yourself in the animal's skin for a long moment,
And experience the overwhelming fear, pain and exhaustion.
Do you like it?
Is that the price the victim has to pay for living,
Just to satisfy you and your companions?
What about the animals' companions, though?
What are they supposed to do?
What do they all feel?
And their families, have you even thought about them?
No.
All that matters to you is the stinking triumph of killing,
And nothing at all goes towards the fox, does it?
Think about the fox.
Everything around the fox.
Others related to the fox.
The innocence of the fox.

Stop!

Kristen Furley

JERUSALEM - TAKE TWO

And did bulldozers dare to invade,
Ploughing up meadows, fields and leas,
And have the axes and chainsaws struck
Annihilating ancient trees,
And were green forests, woods and dells
Forever flattened with no heed
To conservationist's concern,
But satisfied the planner's greed.

Where shelter 'creatures great and small',
When habitats destroyed and lost?
No 'host of golden daffodils'
A sad environmental cost.
Our 'green and pleasant land's' no more
With nature's beauty all around
Tomorrow's children will not see
On England's concrete covered ground.

Jenni J Moores

THE ELEMENTS

Volcanoes erupt
Hurricanes blow
Bush fires start
With a vengeance
Who knows
What tomorrow brings
Automatic weapons
Deadly gas
Twisters, avalanche
All start from scratch
Snow storms
Desert sand
One hundred foot waves
Earthquake
Oil slicks
Rockets in space
Earth, fire, water
The environment
   - Graves -

Patricia Flynn

Mysterious Predator

Stalking our world is a predator leaving no
pebble unturned.

His quest is to trap, exploit and exterminate
the wildlife kingdom and any life form.

Soon we shall find only fragments of dust,
bones turned to powder from the predator's lust.

Footprints now fossilised into pages of history
To erase man from earth, would eradicate this mystery.

Valerie Taber

CHANGING FEAR, CHANGING FREER

       Can you ask the frozen wanderers to melt their hearts,
To open their eyes, when the road they are travelling on exists on
                                    the inside?
Gazing down a highway that tears through your soul,
Looking forward to a life that you could be leading,
You see our present dead on the road,
From the past she's silently bleeding.
It's just you now that's heard screaming.
If you saw the truth,
Then your fragile earth would crack,
Does the prophet seem worth it,
Can you dream your childhood back?
    Does the freedom that you need
Fill you so full of fear,
That you'll greet it with a modern day smile
Should it one day appear?
But have the embers of passion turned to dust
Was that a frown I saw or simply a sneer?
    Tell me where your freedom lies
Tied to the dollar sacred is the game to win
Do you think your heart would hear her knocking
But could you be bothered to let her in?

David Yates

Us, We Are Not Vain

Lonely and frozen, a prison of fear
Upon the draized eyes, a cold hearted tear
The pain of the needle soon takes its cruel toll
The longing of freedom - a mind wasting goal
The hard black stone wall is a captured soul's reign
The scream of pure terror, the freedom from pain
Intense burning flames, flesh cries out 'release'
A dream of the outside, a dream of true peace
The cry of sheer terror, the heart of mere hole
The pain of the needle, yet a numbness of soul
The pain too intense now, the body fades away
But yet, still not allowed to die, a price they should not pay
How much more agony can one soul endure
The health of this innocence grows ever more poor
A glimmer of hope takes over the mind
A certificate of death awaits to be signed
The final dark torture awaits the weak heart
A cocktail of demons rip insides apart
Time to leave pain now, the soul drifts to peace
A prayer for those suffering - so now time to cease
Alas the soul wanders and leaves intense pain
We still claim our innocence
            'Us, we are not vain'

Claire Louise Booker (17)

It's Decorum, Sir

Question not the organisation, sir,
conventions you know
restrict, but how secure
the system! what scope
for initiative did you say?
depends on decisions - ah
decisions - in - the - making
are they fixtures of the future
or a process yet evolving?
take programming - get the gen
analyse - plus data - sift and
sort - consider - reject
revise - add, subtract
The computer will oblige
in case of difficulty -
the final decision will review
last year's decision to
review next year's
indecision - take it or leave it, sir
the system serves the code of decorum
in a manner of speaking, sir
- decidedly so.

Evelyn Leite

INTO THIN AIR

Noticed this squirrel on its side!
As I bike to work, to be on time,
I ride on, pedal pumping to survive,
ride on, into thin air.

Squidgers had it! short-listed,
little legs treadmilling, going nowhere!
Held in sideways stare - of big black crow!
Nowhere to go? Feet, treading air,
treading thin air.

What could I do, to stop nature taking its
course? So, ride on, into early morning sun,
work to be done! Ride on, in acrid traffic air,
just to get there, be there, nothing's fair!
Into thin air.

Anyway, that crow will get his!
One day, when old and weak,
meet his fate to encircled beaks,
his mates will peck him away, then
fly away, into the air,
into thin air.

Forget it! Ride on, under blue skies,
a plane flies, sunlit vapour trails,
maybe to sunny Spain? Holiday bound,
then back to work again,
in a couple of weeks, to encircled beaks.
Now free - in the air, though nothing's fair,
both, hope and despair,
fade into thin air,
all into thin air.

Paul Nicklin

VIOLENT PROTECTION

If you step out of line
or are found in the wrong place,
there'll always be a policeman to re-arrange your face,
but don't bother protesting because you'll be ignored
as they get away with murder as long as it's within the law.
There's no such thing as freedom of speech
try speaking your mind and you'll see what I mean.
Confront authority and you'll be held back
they'll beat you up for being black,
or pick on you for not looking respectable.
The clothes you wear are unacceptable.
Helping old ladies across the road,
teaching youngsters the Green Cross Code,
you can get the impression that they're helping you
and forget the restrictions in everything you do.
They ask so many questions but never answer ours
What happened to Blair Peach, James Kelly and Liddle Towers?

Craig Hetherington

The Party

The police arrived
At next door but one,
To break up the party
And stop all the fun.

We wouldn't have minded,
But we think you'll agree,
It shouldn't have gone on
Till half-past three.

The noise they'd kicked up
Was such a din,
It was obvious they'd had
Too much whisky and gin.

They said they were sorry,
No harm they had meant.
Next time there's a party,
A hall they will rent!

Christine Fraser

OUR FUTURE

My country is beyond repair,
Politics, violence and despair,
Years of evil and religion,
But do people stop to listen -
To what their children have to say,
About their future day.

Yesterday, today and tomorrow,
All will be filled with sorrow,
Today's children lost by hate,
Don't let us follow that same fate.

In our country pride is lost,
Because of the lives it costs,
So please open a new future door,
Our lives are in your hands -
And our futures deserves more.

Carrie Anne Hunter (14)

A Message From A Dying Planet

'I speak to you'
Said the ancient earth to her children
'Have you not heeded the call of your failure'
She spoke softly to the few who were listening and she spilled her love to the fallen
'Wiser still could be your ways'
She prophesied changes to the systems and felt the pangs of a hunger for the dawning was apparent here
'I cannot remain without your love. I am part of you as you are me'
Her words were simple and flowed from her lips like wine
She stood in her skies, a scene of beauty, a different world
The collective of the universe shone into her eyes and my friend she remained
'You have fallen from grace I know that much. Your minds are distracted to your wanton fears. How cannot you see my death drawing near my dear children?'
I wept at her chosen words as I saw the millions turn their backs upon their mother and I thought of the times I spent with her then.
When will we learn? The words leapt to my mind as I wondered where all the flowers had gone!

Alan Pollard

FIRST TIME AROUND - OR WHAT THE ROBOT SAID TO THE PUNK

Stop!
So you're a fully automated, stand up, paid up
Legalised member of the human race.
You can walk and you can run and keep your
Body going at a cracking pace.
You can use up all the energy of the human race
But
Why is it that sometimes you have a long face?
Why
So sad to be a member of the human race?
Surely we have happiness, happiness only to face,
But stop
The word nuclear from your lips, retract, retract,
Once started there is no going back.
This could be the end, the destruction of the human race.
Stop
The word nuclear from your lips and re-adjust the fate of the
Human race.
Now think, go back and tell them what they face.
That crazy happiness pursuit of the human race.

Anne Hadley

INSPIRATION

Not for you the cut and thrust,
Get to work on time or bust,
Not for you the bangs and bashes,
Slaughtered by a thousand crashes,

Not for you a driver's death,
When impressing Jane or Beth,
Not for you the Rock of Ages
At the hand of road-hog rages,

Not for you, pronounced as dead,
When your tyres have no tread,
Not for you the Pearly Gates,
Via the fast lane with your mates,

Forty years without a bump,
Forty years without the hump,
You'll be very hard to match,
Forty years without a scratch!

So for you, my lucky friend,
We've a nicer kind of end,
For it's better, one assumes,
To be killed - by just the fumes!

P J Davies

It Comes To Us All!

Delighted to put a grievance to pen,
When will the young help the old? That's my yen!
Manners of some are non-existent,
Perhaps, deemed *cool* to peers to be non-assistant.

Long ago even unschooled or quite rough,
Would proffer a hand when tasks looked too tough
To the old, disabled, the weak and frail
Volunteered muscle or an arm support handrail.

Who overlooked teaching manners carte-blanche?
Scrapping courtesy, a rude avalanche,
Desist to assist is often witnessed,
Help all life say eager environmentalists.

The young, middle-aged sit glued to their seat,
Forsake pregnant women, loath to unseat,
Ignore old 'un push wheel-chaired spouse uphill,
Impassive to whether effort or pains will kill.

Remember we all become old and grey,
Lack of physical strength looms into play,
Ask not 'Why?' as I overheard today
To a granny's request for aid at the railway.

When one's younger a heavy weight is light,
Two minutes' backing can relieve their plight,
To climb that ladder to hang a curtain,
Replace a light bulb for shrinking aged-boned person.

To all, the next time your might is required
Don't look away, instead be thanked, admired,
Your mother, grandmother may be elsewhere
Sending a prayer for assistance; someone to care.

To any not guilty of indifferent behaviour
Heartfelt thanks for being their saviour.

Hilary Jill Robson

WORDS AND DEEDS

Oh Christmas tree so fresh and clean
When first we smelled your fragrant green
We sprayed turned your green to gold
Put candles -glowing things to hold.

The festive season now has passed.
It's time to throw you at last.
I wish I now could plant you free
Back in the forest, dying tree
But next year, I admit with shame
Our tree will surely be the same.

Jean Bonjour

FREEWHEELING UNSPOKEN WORDS
(For Nick Barber's birthday, November 1997)

To my Dark Chocolate Peppermint

Sweetness . . .
cushion, candy, digging fresh
earth in springtime with bare
hands, falling feathers white
against blue sky, hot pie,
single malt, autumn leaves on
springy untrod woodland floor,
bonfire sparks, twinkles on sunlit lake,
cat weight on sleeping feet,
breath of God waves on barley fields,
hearth, good engine sounds, fresh
water from spring, the perfect curve,
The words that do not yet exist,
You . . .

Beverley Chipp

OUR LAND

Politics and religion, I won't discuss.
But this little poem is a must.
After all we were left this land in trust.
The working class are going bust,
Wanting us all to catch the bus.

The powers on earth, who are they,
Have they the right for this affray.
Fighting here, fighting there,
Don't just stand back and stare.
Let us fight for the things that care.
What has happened to the word 'share'?

Why fight for a little extra land?
It's the people's lives you hold in your hand.
Could it be boredom or just greed
The working class families to feed?
It's us that keeps you off your knees.

Fighting and killing your countrymen,
I would throw you all into the lions' den.
Tyrants you are, but you're not men
Your mother was I, I'd pick up a pen
And sentence you all through the gates of hell.

We are here for a short while that's all.
Who will help cushion the fall?
What do you want, what can you gain
Watching your people scream with pain,
With tears flowing like pouring rain?

Help us have peace throughout the land,
All get together and shake a hand.
We do not own this land we walk,
Do not spoil it with high class talk,
Be real men, among your people walk.

Margaret Sage

Packaging

Clingfilmed society
Everything coated by
A thin transparency
Of plasticised spin
Skilled marketing
Anything that comes with
Creative packaging
And we are taken in
Believe in the binding
Of product integrity
Once pierced and unwinding
Decomposition will begin.

Elizabeth Rigby

Mrs Karakusevic

I'm feeling like a sand castle standing proud upon a beach,
Standing so tall and stately, to the sun I can almost reach.
Then I feel a coldness, the incoming briny around my feet -
- Overwhelmed by the foaming tide I must retreat.
As the waves wash over me I ask, who will know, did anyone see -
- Standing proud upon a beach who will know it was me?
Acclimatised I'm feeling a warmth, a special kind of glow,
I stood once proud upon a beach, and it only matters that I know . . .

Karen Bradley

JUSTICE DENIED

I dreamt of a boy in a uniform
with his arms outstretched to me
he stood in a field of poppies red
where they tied him to a tree
he gazed ahead with dark mute eyes
not sure of where or why
in dawn's cold light they answered
him, this was his day to die.

He was only a boy when he volunteered
and took his sovereign's shilling
he was not to know what lay ahead
of noise, mud and killing
on Flanders Field he fought to win
but weary of battle he lost
as he turned away and tried to hide
he was not to know the cost.

He was not to know in later years
how his family fought, to clear
his name and set him free,
from the stigma it had brought.
The war to end all wars, must
carry the greatest blame, for
in its wake we must all share
its unwitting shame.

As we approach the millennium century
twenty first, let us not take forward
retribution unrehearsed, but seek a
full and final pardon and lay their
souls to rest, in this the last analysis
we face our ultimate test.

Edna M Sarsfield

FREEDOM OF SPEECH

'The tongue is mightier than the sword'
Where freedom is a precious word.
The fight goes on to make one heard
Above the clamour, undeterred.

The power of the printed word
In global matters, interfered.
Flouting the law by devious means,
Things are never what they seem.

In countries torn by civil war:
Freedom of speech denied by law,
A man must think before he speaks
Or lose the freedom which he seeks.

Muriel Hughes

Untitled

The war will never be over
As long as there are people who remember
Or people who have been taught
They humour us, throw us the occasional victory
But we never really win
They are in control
And they perpetuate the lie
We can pretend things have changed
That they hear our voices
Perhaps they do hear
But they don't listen
All they can see is danger
Fear is what keeps them strong
The world is black and white
There is no equal
Only controller and controlled
And it will never be different
Unless we educate our children
Teach them the right way
And leave behind the relics of the past.

Emma Pearce

VICTORY?

What is this festering canker now I find,
Swelling with pus of hatred for my fellow man,
Poisoning my mind, feeding the bloody hand
That wields the bottle, paints the wall,
Flies the flag, the banner, black or bright,
Rallies to the baying call? Plants the bomb?

Oh awful, bloody sight,
What is this tribal barrier whence we fell?

Is there no Heaven? Only Hell?
Evil - has it already won? It bids
'Go forth and multiply
Multiply, ever loving son.'

Ann Stewart

SUBMISSIONS INVITED
SOMETHING FOR EVERYONE

POETRY NOW '99 - Any subject, any style, any time.

'99 - Strictly women, have your say the female way!

STRONGWORDS '99 - Warning! Age restriction, must be between 16-24, opinionated and have strong views. (Not for the faint-hearted)

All poems no longer than 30 lines.
Always welcome! No fee!
Cash Prizes to be won!

Mark your envelope (eg *Poetry Now*) **'99**
Send to:
Forward Press Ltd
1-2 Wainman Road, Woodston,
Peterborough, PE2 7BU

**OVER £10,000 POETRY PRIZES
TO BE WON!**

Judging will take place in October 1999